Introduction to

Introduction to Philosophy of Education

JAMES GRIBBLE

University of Melbourne

Allyn and Bacon, Inc.   Boston

Seventh printing . . . November, 1973

Preface

THIS BOOK is intended to provide a starting
point for students of philosophy of education who have no
previous philosophical training. Most authors of available texts
either take for granted that their readers will know something
about philosophy or they attempt to introduce their readers to
"general philosophy" and then move on to philosophy of education. The first assumption is usually misplaced since people who
are preparing to be teachers rarely study philosophy. The
second approach attempts too much; even if the time were
available in schools and colleges of education to tackle the
various fields of "general philosophy" it is doubtful that this is
the best way of introducing the subject to students of education. The ethical, logical and epistemological issues are opened
up more relevantly through the educational problems.

An introduction to any subject should be a stimulus to discussion and to further reading and thought. Therefore, my endeavor is not to instruct, but to provoke argument, without
which philosophy is dead. To this end, each topic is treated
with maximum directness, in order to get students *doing* philosophical analysis of educational concepts and arguments rather
than merely reading *about* the activity. Although each topic is
presented so that it can be read and discussed independently,
the book has two or three central arguments which, it is hoped,
provide continuity and coherence.

My debt to Professor R. S. Peters and Professor P. H. Hirst
will be obvious to any reader familiar with their works. If the
only virtue of this book is to lead its readers on to work such as
theirs it will have served a useful function. Indeed, it should
be taken as merely a starting point in the subject or its purpose
will be misunderstood. I am also very grateful to Professor
L. R. Perry who read an earlier version of the manuscript and
who offered helpful criticism and advice.

JAMES GRIBBLE

Contents

•

1

Philosophy
and
Education

(A) THE RELATIONSHIP BETWEEN
PHILOSOPHY AND EDUCATION

IN RECENT YEARS there has been a revolu-
tion in philosophy of education, following on the "revolution in
philosophy" which was inaugurated by the work of Wittgenstein a few decades ago. Until quite recently philosophy of
education was merely a study of the works of the "great
educators"—such courses would have been more aptly described as courses in the history of educational ideas, even
though some attempt was usually made to relate the ideas of
such men as Plato and Rousseau to modern educational problems. Undoubtedly such courses were often valuable, and familiarity with the views of such men still is an important part
of philosophy of education as it is now understood. But such
familiarity is emphatically only a part of what is meant by
philosophy of education.

It is much easier to say what philosophy of education is not than to say what it is. Most general comment about philosophical techniques is pretty worthless. This is partly because the question, "What is philosophy?" is itself a widely disputed philosophical issue. It is much more important to recognize the problems involved in philosophical analysis than to look for an easily applied formula. Rather than make summaries of what philosophy is (or is supposed to be) we would profit more from seeing how philosophers proceed when they are on the job. In the next section we will examine R. S. Peters' analysis of what is meant by speaking of "education," and part of our discussion will be to demonstrate philosophical technique. For although Peters' analysis is a fine example of what the working educational philosopher does, it is certainly not possible to derive from it an easily applied formula. On the contrary it raises one or two very interesting questions about the nature of philosophical analysis. Being able to see such questions is in itself a big step towards seeing how philosophy works.

With these qualifications in mind we may nevertheless make a few fairly careful remarks about philosophical analysis in education, for it would be unfortunate if the result of being too guarded were to lead anyone into thinking that philosophy were a kind of esoteric cult practiced only by its initiates. The revolution in philosophy of education is characterized mainly by a new concern with the *meaning* of concepts which are recurrent in educational debate and with the logic of the justifications which are offered in educational debate. R. S. Peters, who has been mainly responsible for the revolution in philosophy of education in Britain, constantly recurs to the Socratic questions, "What do you mean?" and "How do you know?" It is essential to ask these questions in educational debates where such concepts as "freedom," "equality," "development," "needs," "abilities," "knowledge" and so on are prevalent—essential even though we may be able to apply these concepts in concrete situations. Gilbert Ryle's point about mental-conduct epithets is relevant to these concepts too:

It is one thing to know how to apply such concepts, quite another to know how to correlate them with one another and with concepts of other sorts. Many people can talk sense with concepts but cannot talk sense about them; they know by practice how to operate with concepts, anyhow inside familiar fields, but they cannot state the logical relations governing their use. They are like people who know their way about their own parish, but cannot construct or read a map of it, much less a map of the region or continent in which their parish lies.[1]

In Ryle's view, the job is not to increase what we know, but to "rectify the logical geography of the knowledge which we already possess."

This is certainly the prior task in philosophy of education. But the logical mapping of concepts in education is not done simply for its own sake. The philosopher of education is not content, for example, simply to point out that the concept of "equality" may imply treating people differently—it is his job to go on and examine the implications of his analysis for the content of education. In this case he would want to deny that treating people "equally" implied that everyone should have the same education. But he would oppose differentiation of treatment where no relevant differences could be pointed to in those being educated. (This point will receive extended treatment in a later chapter.) In such ways he moves from the analysis of concepts into the thick of the educational infighting. And inroads into the jungle of unanalyzed verbiage which has for so long made the study of education an academic wilderness are already being made by philosophers intent on questions of educational practice.

In his analysis of the concept of "education"—obviously a key concept in our field of inquiry—Peters looks for the rules or criteria according to which we employ or do not properly employ the concept of "education." This procedure is one of the fundamental techniques of "conceptual analysis." When philos-

[1] Gilbert Ryle, *The Concept of Mind* (Middlesex, England: G. B. Penguin Books, Ltd., 1963) pp. 10f.

ophers ask, "What does x mean?" they are asking, "What are the rules or criteria for using this concept?" This procedure is grounded in Wittgenstein's later philosophy. The meaning of a word, as Wittgenstein points out, is its use in discourse. Any attempted definition of a word will include a list of criteria[2] for its use. But just what *are* the criteria for the use of such concepts as "education," "freedom," "knowledge" and so on may be very difficult to decide. If the search should seem frustrating sometimes, or agreement difficult to reach, it is worth recalling that Wittgenstein also points out that ". . . in general we don't use language according to strict rules—it hasn't been taught us by means of strict rules either."

It is important to distinguish the analytic technique under discussion from defining terms. When a philosopher asks "What does x mean?", he is not asking for a definition of x—at least not in the dictionary sense of "definition." He wants to know what are the criteria for the use of the term x. This is not usually what is expected when we ask for the definition of a term; the philosophic analysis of meaning may add to or even conflict with dictionary definitions. An example of such conflict may be seen on page 32 where we reject part of the dictionary account of the meaning of "indoctrination." To give a brief illustration of such analysis, let us consider the concept of "communication." The dictionary definition is, "Act of imparting; information given; intercourse." Now this definition does not state, it only implies one of the most obvious criteria for using the term "communication"—that it be between two or more people or creatures. While we may sometimes speak of communication with oneself, a philosopher would describe this as a metaphorical or "secondary" sense of the term. It is "parasitic" on our understanding its "primary" usage as being between two creatures. We could not understand what is meant by "communication with oneself" unless we had a prior under-

---

[2] We are ignoring a number of complexities here. Those interested in following them through might consult, for example, L. Wittgenstein's *Blue Book* (Oxford: Oxford University Press, 1964) pp. 24f, and *Philosophical Investigations* (Oxford: Oxford University Press, 1963) Sections 321 and 322. See also "Wittgenstein's Concept of a Criterion," Carl Wellman, *Philosophical Review*, Vol. LXXI, 1962.

standing of what communication between two creatures meant. It is nonsense to speak of communicating with a lamppost. The man in the song who was reputed to have talked to the trees was doing no such thing. He was "talking at" them, perhaps, but he was not communicating with them, which is what we mean by "talking to" them. (We may safely ignore the disturbing overtones of a "communicating door" except to note that there is another range of "secondary" meanings in such contexts.)

Furthermore, "communication" is what philosophers (since Ryle) call an "achievement" verb. You cannot be said to communicate without getting something across. Whereas, as every teacher knows, there is a sense of "teaching" and of "education" in which no one may understand, and yet we may slump back in the staffroom and say, "Well, I taught that class as well as I could, but no one understood." "Teaching" is being used here in its "task" (or "attempt") sense, and the concept of "education" may be used in a similar way. (The most vivid example of this distinction between the "task" and "achievement" senses of some verbs is "fishing." We often see people sitting day after day on the end of a pier dangling a line into the water with never a sign of a fish. But if you ask them what they're doing they will say surprisedly, "Fishing." This is emphatically the "task" sense of the verb. We ought to observe, too, that if no one had *ever* caught fish by dangling baited lines into the water it would not be called fishing. Verbs only develop a "task" sense if an activity is sometimes successful.)

This brief analysis of the concept of "communication" ran through some fairly straightforward applications of such phrases as "primary meaning," "secondary meaning," "parasitic upon," "criteria," "achievement sense," and "task sense." These are terms which will be frequently employed in the discussions to follow. But as we shall see, the application of such terms is by no means always straightforward. When we raise questions about the applicability of such terms we are raising questions about the nature of philosophical analysis—about the appropriateness of philosophical procedures themselves. The fact that such questions arise very frequently generated our earlier remarks that there are no easily applied formulas for teaching or learning how to do philosophical analysis. Apart from this, the following main points have been made:

* There has been a revolution in philosophy of education in that the concern is now with analysis of the way concepts are used in educational debate and with the logic of justifications which are offered in arguments about education.

* Philosophical analysis in education is not carried on just for its own sake but primarily in order to clear the ground for making a wide variety of practical decisions about the conduct of education.

* Philosophical analysis of concepts is not to be confused with the definition of terms in dictionaries.

(B) THE CONCEPT OF EDUCATION

R. S. Peters' analysis of the concept of "education" is instructive as a fine example of the sort of procedure which it is essential to grasp in order to do philosophy of education. And as we shall see, it raises several interesting questions about the nature of philosophical analysis. But before we see how his procedure (and some of his content) might be questioned we shall present Peters' main arguments as directly as possible.[3] Peters' analysis of the concept is the most challenging to be found, and it is the starting point of a whole network of argument which follows up the ethical, psychological, and epistemological assumptions of the analysis. He argues that there are three criteria which an activity must satisfy if it is to be called "education."

(1) The first and most important criterion is that something of value must be passed on in an activity which is properly to be called "education." In some ways this is obvious —for example, if we were to train a class in the art of torture or in burglary nothing of value would be passed on and we would not call such activities educational. But these are examples of activities which are not merely valueless, but are actually

[3] See R. S. Peters' Inaugural Lecture, "Education as Initiation," in *Philosophical Analysis and Education*, ed. R. D. Archambault (London: Routledge and Kegan Paul, Ltd., 1965) pp. 88–101. By permission of Routledge and Kegan Paul Ltd. and Humanities Press, Inc.

harmful. What about activities of a neutral sort, which are neither harmful nor valuable? Consider this example. A teacher of French has to take a class while the teacher of German is away sick. Not knowing what to do with the class, he puts up a list of irregular French verbs on the blackboard and gets the class to learn them by heart. The class has never studied French before and the verbs are meaningless symbols to them. Nothing of value is passed on, and although the children have learned nothing harmful, they have not been engaged in an activity which could be called "education." But if this is true, there are a number of skills which we teach children which are not properly "education." For example, teaching a child the skills of reading and writing may not be an educational activity. These activities are not valuable in themselves, but they make possible other activities which are valuable in themselves. If we taught a child to read and write, but he never read or wrote anything after he had mastered these skills, we could not say that he had been educated. These skills are necessary preconditions for engaging in a number of activities which are valuable, such as science, history, literature and so on. But since the skills are not valuable in themselves, since they are not intrinsically valuable, the activity of mastering these skills is not properly an educational activity. This distinction between activities which are intrinsically valuable or valuable in themselves, and activities which are only instrumentally valuable, or valuable as means to an end, is of key importance. For only the former—the intrinsically valuable activities—may properly be educational activities. It always makes sense to ask what is the *aim* of learning such skills as reading and writing or the multiplication tables, for to ask for aims is to ask for the valuable ends which will be achieved by performing activities which are not in themselves valuable. By asking what the aims are, we are asking what extrinsic value will be achieved.

There is, however, a misconception involved in asking what is the aim of education. For part of what we mean by education is that something of value is being passed on. In order to elucidate this point, Peters employs an analogy with the concept of "reform." It is not the aim of reform to make someone better. Part of what is meant by reforming someone is that they are being made better. Similarly, it is not an aim of education to engage in certain activities in order to achieve worthwhile objectives, for part of what is meant by education is that worthwhile activities are being engaged in. If there is no other way of justifying teaching something to children than by saying that it will help them to achieve something *else* thought to be valuable, then the teaching is not properly an educational activity.

It should be noted, however, that "education" and "teaching" may refer to the attempt to pass on what is worthwhile even if the attempt is not successful. It was pointed out before that we may say, "I taught that class as well as I could but no one understood" and that "teaching" is here being used in its "attempt" or "task" sense and "education" can be used in a similar way. But both concepts are most frequently employed to refer to a more or less successful activity, i.e. their "achievement" sense is the primary sense. Something of value must ordinarily or usually be successfully passed on if the activities are to be part of education, and something must ordinarily be learned if an activity is properly to be called "teaching."

But perhaps we are moving too rapidly, and perhaps the dismissal of the view that education has "aims" was rather too peremptory. After all, talk about the aims of education has been going on for a long time. Nevertheless much of this talk has been misleading. Usually when people say that we must formulate our educational aims they mean that we must find out what valuable ends of an extrinsic kind are to be achieved by engaging in the study of literature, science, history and so on. The sort of model that they have in mind is of something to be gone through in order that some desirable outcome will ensue. And while this model is appropriate to a number of skills which are usually learned very early on, it is entirely inappropriate to see an engagement in activities which are valuable in themselves as merely the means to achieving extrinsic ends. One familiar example of this kind of thinking is the view held by a number of sociologists and men in the street, that education has vocational aims—that education is the means of providing people with the training which will enable them to get a suitable job. The educational system is viewed as a vast sorting system, with people dropping out at various points and going into jobs which are appropriate to the level they have attained. Or education may be viewed by economists and politicians as a means to increasing productivity.

Now it would be foolish to deny that a *result* of education may be that productivity is increased or that people are sorted into appropriate vocational niches. It would be equally foolish to deny that as a result of education, employment is provided for large numbers of people in the building and printing industries. What must be denied is that education is instrumental in attaining these results—which is what is implied if we speak of them as aims of education. The study of science is obviously related to the provision of trained manpower and to productivity, but these effects are not what makes science an educational activity. Instead, it is the intrinsic value of science which makes it an educational activity—science is a way of understanding the world, of making sense of experience, regardless of the practical uses to which this understanding may be put. It is just a bonus if the development of a particular form of understanding has useful extrinsic results.

In case it is thought that we are arguing that science is ultimately instrumental—that the aim of doing science is to develop understanding—we should point out that part of what is *meant* by doing science is the development of (scientific) understanding—that this is a way of referring to that which makes it an intrinsically valuable activity. It is not referring to an aim which is extrinsic to science.

(2) Nevertheless there is much that could go on in schools under the name of "science" or "history" or "literature" which need not be educational. For example, if just *one* of these subjects were taught in a very narrow and limited way, we may want to question whether this is properly to be called "education." Thus you may train a mathematician to be extremely proficient at making highly complicated moves in an

esoteric system of symbols. But surely we would want to ask, if that is *all* he can do, whether he is properly to be described as an educated man. And this qualification brings out the second criterion which any activity must satisfy if it is to be called an educational activity: there must be what Peters calls a "wide cognitive perspective." This is also a very general criterion and it may be difficult to say how wide the cognitive perspective must be if an activity is to be called an educational activity. But such activities as mathematics, science, history, literature and so on are central to education not only because they are valuable in themselves, but also because they may widen and deepen one's view of countless other matters.

If an historian never saw the way history related to morality or to sociology or to literature, but was concerned with past events as if they were entirely removed from other forms of understanding or the conduct of living, could we regard him as educated? Imagine, for example, an historian of the French Revolution who was surprised if you told him that a study of this period led one to think about freedom and equality and social justice, and who said he never thought about such things, he was only concerned with the facts. This may be a valuable concern, and we may be glad that someone is burrowing away accumulating information, but if we were asked if such limited activities were characteristic of an educated man, wouldn't we hesitate? Wouldn't it be more appropriate to say that he had been highly trained? (Assuming that he is efficient at digging up information.)

We speak instead of *training* a man in circumscribed skills. For example you train a man to carry out certain performances with a machine. You train a pilot or a mechanic. Similarly we often say that a man is a trained historian or a trained scientist. But such a man need not be educated. We do not speak of educating a man as a scientist or as an historian any more than we speak of educating a man as a cook or as a builder. Instead, we reserve the term "education" for a range of activities which broaden and deepen our understanding—in other words, have a wide cognitive perspective. If this were not a necessary part of what is meant by education, it would be acceptable to speak of educating a man as an historian or as a barber.

(3) The other condition which any educational activity must satisfy, besides being valuable in itself and related to other activities thought to be valuable, is that those who are engaged in it must come to *care* about what they are doing. Consider an example where the first two criteria are satisfied. A man has completed a university course in English, history and economics—a wide range of valuable activities. But having finished his examinations he breathes a deep sigh of relief, says "Thank God that's over," and spends all his time from then on reading comics and playing cards. He never again shows any sign of interest in literature or in political or economic affairs and says that he couldn't care less about all that stuff. Could we say, then, that he was educated? What is there to distinguish him from someone who had never engaged in the activities at all? The letters after his name, perhaps, but they don't matter. We might say that he knew a lot, or had been highly trained. But if he does not care at all about what he knows, surely we must deny that he is educated.

Following Peters, it has been argued that "education" implies that an activity satisfies three criteria:

(1) That the activity is valuable in itself.

(2) That the activity is associated with other activities so that there is a wide cognitive perspective, i.e., it is seen to relate to other ways of understanding and experiencing.

(3) That those who are engaged in the activity come to care for it, come to think that it is worth doing.

Having thus put Peters' analysis as directly as possible as a challenge to our assumptions about the concept of "education," we ought to consider some of the ways in which the gauntlet might be taken up. When Peters presented a version of the foregoing analysis as part of a paper to an international seminar on philosophy and education in Toronto in 1966 it was subjected to some stimulating criticism by Professor Woods and Professor Dray of the University of Toronto. The discussion suggested two main questions which we might put to Peters:

1. What does he mean when he speaks of a "conceptual connection" between "education" and engaging in "worthwhile" activities? This question is important in view of the fact that we have offered Peters' analysis as the sort of procedure which is important to grasp if we are to do philosophy of education. Peters maintained, in the discussion, that the conceptual connections with which he is concerned are not as tight as those between, for example, the concept of being a "bachelor" and that of being "unmarried." In this case there is a straightforward contradiction if someone is asserted to be a bachelor and also to be married. (The connection is often called an "analytic" one by philosophers. An "analytic" relationship between terms simply implies that part of what is meant by one term is to be found in the other, so that to assert one and deny the other is to be self-contradictory.[4])

In Peters' view, philosophers are legitimately interested not only in logical inconsistencies as obvious as contradictions but also in cases of logical "oddness" or "quaintness." Why then does Peters insist in *Ethics and Education*, that "it would be a logical contradiction to say that a man had been educated but that he had in no way changed for the better, or that in educating his son a man was attempting nothing that was worthwhile."[5] While we can make the weaker claim, that it would be an "odd" thing for someone to say, we can surely envisage a man who thinks book learning and middle-class culture to be a way of messing up lower-class boys and alienating them from their family and friends. He might well say that his son had been educated but had changed for the worse. And while it may sound rather odd, it could hardly be said to be a logical contradiction. If we imagine a father for Jimmy Porter in Osborne's play *Look Back in Anger*, might he not say without

---

4 The concept of "analyticity" has been the subject of much philosophical dispute. The sense of "analytic" used in this text is what Professor D. A. T. Gasking calls the "vulgar" sense.

5 From *Ethics and Education* by R. S. Peters. © George Allen & Unwin, Ltd., 1966, p. 25. Reprinted by permission of George Allen & Unwin, Ltd. and Scott, Foresman and Company.

self-contradiction (though perhaps not accurately) that Jimmy's education had simply made him into an angry young layabout?

In the seminar discussion, Peters meets the suggestion that a father might say that his son had turned out to be a snob because of (rather than in spite of) his education by observing that he would be using "education" in an external descriptive sort of way, like a person who says of a criminal, "He is reformed all right; but as a result he just takes it out on his wife." And Peters asks if this would show that "reform" is not connected with making people better. Peters undoubtedly has a point here, and there is, surely, a connection between "education" and doing something worthwhile. But the connection seems to be weaker than an analytic one, i.e., it need not be self-contradictory to claim that someone had been educated but had not changed for the better.

2. Is Peters really fabricating a concept of education out of his vision of what people ought to become and hoping that its circulation will have a beneficial effect upon schools? Those who read Peters often seem to think this, and in the seminar discussion Peters admits that he "might have tightened up the concept a bit." Presumably an example of the "tightening" is the one we have just examined—the connection between "education" and "worthwhileness" is somewhat looser than Peters maintains. But he quite rightly resists the implication that his analysis is related to "a vision of what people ought to become." Peters points out that his analysis is "rather content-free," and adds:

> I take the concept of "education" to be almost as unspecific in terms of content as something like "good" or "worthwhile" with the notion of "transmission of" or "initiation into" prefixed to it. It is slightly more specific than "good" because of the cognitive criteria to do with depth and breadth of understanding and awareness that I suggested also went with it.[6]

[6] See R. S. Peters, "Aims of Education—A Conceptual Enquiry," in *Philosophy and Education, Proceedings of the International Seminar, March 23–25, 1966* (Toronto: The Ontario Institute for Studies in Education, 1967).

No one concerned with education can afford to ignore this debate about the nature of "education." The practicing teacher is continually afflicted by lecturers, books and articles which refer blithely and unthinkingly to our "aims." Educational policy makers customarily begin their reports with lengthy and usually vapid statements of the "aims" of education. Educational sociologists frequently confuse analysis of the "function" of education with analysis of its "aims," and they usually ignore Peters' point that "socialization" is too general to specify those worthwhile characteristics that are distinctive of "education." Educational psychologists who are fond of referring to such "aims" of education as "mental health," "self-realization," "needs-satisfaction," "growth" and so on clearly need to do some homework on what is meant by "education." (See chapter 4 for an analysis of these "psychological" concepts in educational discussion.) Educational historians are not directly affected in these ways, but it would be interesting to relate Peters' ideas to the tradition of thinking about education which Newman and Arnold represented in the nineteenth century. Some of the connections with Arnold's views are made in the introduction to *Matthew Arnold*,[7] edited by the present writer. The connection with Newman is suggested, for example, by the passage which appears below as a subject for discussion.

BASIC READING

PETERS, R. S., "Education as Initiation," *Philosophical Analysis and Education*, ed. R. D. Archambault. London: Routledge & Kegan Paul, Ltd., 1965.

———, *Authority, Responsibility and Education*, Chapter 8. London: Allen & Unwin, Ltd., 1963.

FURTHER REFERENCES

PETERS, R. S., "Mental Health as an Educational Aim," *Aims in Education*, ed. T. H. B. Hollins, particularly pp. 83–90. Manchester, England: Manchester University Press, 1964.

———, *Ethics and Education*, Part I. London: Allen & Unwin, Ltd., 1966.

[7] James Gribble (ed.), *Matthew Arnold* (London: Collier-Macmillan Ltd., 1967).

DISCUSSION/ESSAY TOPICS

* Is education worthwhile?

* "All I say is, call things by their right names and do not confuse together items which are essentially different. . . . Recreations are not education; accomplishments are not education. Do not say, the people must be educated, when, after all, you only mean amused, refreshed, soothed, put into good spirits and good humour, or kept from vicious excesses. I do not say that such amusements, such occupations of mind, are not a great gain; but they are not education. . . . Stuffing birds or playing stringed instruments is an elegant pastime, and a resource to the idle, but it is not education; it does not form or cultivate the intellect. Education is a high word; it is the imparting of knowledge, and it is the imparting of knowledge in proportion to that preparation." (*On the Scope and Nature of University Education*, pp. 136–7. Cardinal John Henry Newman, London: Everyman, 1965.)

Compare this analysis of "education" with R. S. Peters' analysis.

* "Peters' central contention is that the more general problems of education are not means/ends problems at all. . . . The more general aims of education, such objects as 'self-realization', 'character', 'citizenship', are, in his view, neither goals nor end products. Like 'happiness' they are high-sounding ways of talking about doing some things rather than others and of doing them in a certain manner. Statements about the aims of education are better to be understood as expressing views about *how* rather than *what* we should teach, views about the procedure rather than the content of education. Values are involved in education less in the shape of goals or end products than as principles implicit in certain manners of proceeding." (R. F. Atkinson, "Instruction and Indoctrination," ed. R. D. Archambault, *Philosophical Analysis and Education.* © 1965, by Routledge & Kegan Paul, Ltd., London. Reprinted by permission of Routledge & Kegan Paul, Ltd. and Humanities Press, Inc.)

Is this Peters' central contention? If so, how does Peters support it?

Education
and
Teaching

WE NEVER SAY at the end of a hard day's teaching, "I've been educating flat out today." And we could no more look into classrooms as we walk down school corridors and see someone educating than we would ask Mr. Jones, the science teacher, if he educated 4B in period 6. What we usually see teachers doing when we look into classrooms is teaching, instructing, training, drilling, even perhaps indoctrinating or conditioning. When do we speak of "educating" children, then? One occasion might be after a series of demonstration lessons by a very good teacher, when we might sum up our admiration for all his activities by saying, "Yes, he's really educating those boys." Perhaps in moments of euphoria we might even think of our own teaching, when we look back over a good year's work, that we have been educating children. All these examples reflect Peters' point that when we speak of "education" and "educating" we are not referring to any particular form of teaching such as "instruction," "training," "indoctrination" and so on. What we are doing when we speak of "education" and "educating" is saying that a whole range of particular teaching activities comes up to certain standards. As Peters maintains, "education" implies criteria for judging the worth of a variety of particular teaching activities; it does not imply that any particular kind of teaching activity has been performed. When we form a judgment after watching or performing various teaching activities that what is going on deserves to be called "educating" we mean that the net effect is one which satisfies the three criteria which have been outlined. We have evidence that what is being taught is worthwhile in itself, that it is not narrow or limited in its cognitive range, and that the pupils are beginning to care for the activities in which the teacher is engaging them.

On the other hand, many of the activities which we engage in with children may be described as "teaching" activities, even though they are concerned with material which is not worthwhile in itself, which is of limited cognitive range and about which the pupils don't care. The main point to be advanced in this section is that there is only one necessary condition which an activity must satisfy if it is to be correctly described as a case of "teaching"—this is that the pupils *learn* something of what the teacher intends them to learn. (It will be plain that this condition only applies when "teaching" is being used in its "achievement" sense. In its "task" sense, it is true, we may say "I taught that class but they learned nothing." But even here there is an obvious intention that the teaching activity was designed to get the class to learn something. It is a logical contradiction—or a joke—to claim to have taught something with no intention that someone learn what is being taught.)

It is an extraordinary fact that a point so obvious as this has been misunderstood by the leading writers on education over the last few years. Peters, for example, maintains that ". . . teaching involves discussion and explanation as methods for bringing about an ability to discuss and explain on the part of the learner."[1] Peters goes on to deny that "instruction" or "training" are "teaching activities" unless they are undertaken with the intention of bringing about rational understanding and are "accompanied by the appropriate encouragement and explanation." Similarly, Scheffler, who accepts the view that "teaching" is an activity which is aimed at the achievement of learning, wants to add that it must be "practised in such a manner as to respect the student's intellectual integrity and capacity for independent judgement."[2] Scheffler claims that this second criterion ". . . differentiates the activity of teaching from such other activities as propaganda, conditioning, suggestion and indoctrination, which are aimed at modifying the person but strive at all costs to avoid a genuine engagement of his judgement on underlying issues."

Now there are important distinctions to be made between "*education*" and such activities as "propaganda," "conditioning" and "indoctrination." For these activities all necessarily fail to satisfy one or more of the criteria for calling an activity educational. But they are all particular forms of *teaching*. "Teaching" is what Ryle calls a "polymorphous concept"—it is a ragbag concept which may embrace all those techniques mentioned by Scheffler as well as "training" and "instructing."

Scheffler's reason for wanting to exclude "propaganda," "conditioning" and "indoctrination" from the family of activities headed "teaching" is that they "strive at all costs to avoid a genuine engagement of [the pupil's] judgment on underlying issues." And this raises the important question about the single criterion which we are advancing. We have claimed that the only necessary condition for an activity to be "teaching" is that the pupils learn something of what the teacher intends them to learn. But can we say that someone who had been conditioned or indoctrinated has learned something? What is meant by "learning?" Scheffler says that a special kind of learning has to

---

[1] Peters, *Ethics and Education,* p. 40.
[2] Israel Scheffler, "Philosophical Models of Teaching," *Harvard Educational Review,* Vol. 35, No. 3 (Summer 1965), p. 131.

take place if we are to claim that "teaching" has taken place—it must take into account the subject's capacity for "independent judgement." Presumably this is why Peters insists on discussion and explanation as necessary characteristics of "teaching."

But if this were so, it would mean that there was something wrong with saying "I taught my dog to jump through a hoop," or for a Catholic or a Communist to say, "I taught my four-year-old child the doctrines of the Church" or of Marx and Engels. Now it may be more precise to speak in the first case of "training" the dog and in the second case of "indoctrinating" the child. But it seems absurd to suggest that there is anything wrong with calling these activities "teaching"—although no appeal can be made to a dog's independent judgment and no appeal may be made to the child's.

In the face of this, Scheffler and Peters might alter the emphasis of their argument. Instead of insisting that "teaching" is defined in terms of certain sorts of procedure, they might try to define it with reference to the nature of the beliefs which are passed on by teachers. They might concede that the only necessary condition for testing whether or not teaching has taken place is to see if that which was taught has been learned. But they might insist that we can only speak of "teaching" and "learning" where the beliefs which are passed on are true or rational beliefs. For example, they might say that if Johnny comes home from school one day after a member of the Flat Earth Society has convinced him that the earth is flat it could not be claimed that he has *learned* that it is flat, since it is, in fact, round.

In school situations, "learning" is customarily associated with acquiring true or rational beliefs. But in a case such as this, we do not say that Johnny has learned nothing. He has acquired a false belief—he has learned to view the shape of the earth as being other than it actually is. The important residual point which could be salvaged from Peters' and Scheffler's arguments is that Johnny must have some understanding of the proposition "the earth is flat" and some notion of the evidence for this proposition if we are to say that he has learned that the earth is flat. There is a vital distinction between learning to repeat the proposition parrot-fashion and acquiring the belief that the earth is flat. We could not say that Johnny has learned that the earth is flat or that he has been taught that it is flat if all he can do is repeat the proposition without understanding it or without having some notion of the evidence for the belief—for example, "it *looks* flat."

This point may make us very hesitant to refer to some forms of indoctrination as cases of "teaching." It does not any longer seem absurd to wonder if we should say "I *taught* my four-year-old child the doctrines of the Church" or of Marx and Engels. For a four-year-old child is not likely to be able to understand these doctrines or to be able to follow the evidence for them. He is more likely to be capable only of reciting the doctrines parrot-fashion than to have acquired beliefs about the class-struggle or the Trinity. This would lead us to deny that he had learned or been taught the doctrines. But the indoctrinator is *also* dissatisfied if his subject does not acquire the beliefs he is trying to pass on. The indoctrinator wants some degree of understanding in his pupil of the beliefs he is transmitting, some notion of the evidence for them, and insofar as this is so, then his pupils may be said to be learning the doctrines and the indoctrinator to be engaged in a form of teaching. It is only in extreme cases when the subject is not encouraged to understand the doctrine or to see the evidence for it that we would question whether the doctrine is being learned or taught. But then we would also doubt whether this was indoctrination at all.

There are reasons for being much more hesitant about saying that "conditioning" is a case of "teaching." There is something odd about saying that a dog has been taught to salivate at the sound of a bell. And we will shortly argue that this is because it is a bit odd to say that a dog has *learned* to salivate at the sound of a bell. The dog has developed some regularity of response, but we feel the concept of "learning" has been excessively stretched to accommodate conditioned responses. In the immediately following sections we will also attempt a more detailed analysis of "training," "instructing" and "indoctrinating." So far our conclusion is the general one that each of these may be properly described as forms of teaching insofar as they are intended to promote the end that someone *learn* what is being transmitted. No other criterion apart from this is a valid one.

We shall conclude this section by returning to the comparison with which we began, between "education" and "teaching." Two points may be made.

(1) "Teaching" in some form seems to be necessary for "education" to take place. Can we think of any way of educating someone that does not involve some form of teaching him? It has sometimes been thought that the "discovery method" is a method which obviates the need to teach—the children find out things for themselves. But as R. F. Dearden[3] has pointed out, it is not by chance that these so-called discoveries are made, but as a result of the teacher's contrivance in "structuring the environment" or practicing "discovery methods." The discoveries which are made are those which the teacher wants the children to discover—it is a covert form of teaching.

(2) "Teaching" and "education" are confused by Professor Bantock in his *Education and Values*. He argues[4] that by "teaching" we necessarily imply that what is being transmitted is valuable or worthwhile, which is to say that "teaching" shares one of the criteria which distinguish educational activities. Professor Bantock's claims that a school for pickpockets could not be said to "teach" its pupils, insofar as what is being transmitted is not valuable or worthwhile. The fact that the activity seems not to be an intrinsically valuable activity means that what is going on in the school could hardly be "education." But surely the young pickpockets are being "taught" to pick pockets.

It is vital to get this distinction between "education" and "teaching" right. So often when sociologists, psychologists and politicians speak about "education" they mean *whatever* teach-

---

[3] "Instruction and Learning by Discovery," *The Concept of Education*, ed. R. S. Peters (London: Routledge and Kegan Paul, Ltd., 1967) pp. 142–44.
[4] G. H. Bantock, *Education and Values* (London: Faber and Faber, Ltd., 1965) pp. 167–68.

ing and learning goes on in schools. But "teaching" and "education" are by no means equivalent concepts, and much that is taught and learned fails to come up to the standards which are implied by speaking of "education." Insofar as "teaching" is merely "instructing" or "training" or "indoctrinating" it fails to satisfy one or more of the criteria for "education" to be taking place. We will examine each of these concepts to see in what ways they fall short of the standards implied by speaking of "education."

TRAINING

We have described the distinction between "education" and "training" by pointing out that while we may speak of training a man in a narrowly conceived or circumscribed activity, we reserve the term "education" for processes which have a wide cognitive perspective, where there is a more than specialistic interest. We don't *educate* a man to run a machine, to ride a bike or to swim—we speak of "training" when we teach skills. Thus we speak of "training" a dog. But it is absurd to speak of "educating" a dog.

There is a rather different sense of "training," in which we may speak of training a man as a biologist or an historian, and these activities do seem closer to educational activities. They satisfy the first criterion for "education" in that their concern with the development of understanding is some evidence of their worthwhileness. But although there is a wider cognitive perspective in biology or history than there is in riding bikes or running machines, it is not wide enough for us to refer to the training of a man in these activities as "education." We do not speak of "educating" a man as a biologist or as an historian. If, however, we increase the range of activities then it ceases to sound odd to speak of "education." If we say, "My education was in the sciences" or "My education was in the humanities," then the concept fits. This point may be useful in answering a question which arose earlier. When we maintained that one of the criteria for "educational" activities was that there be a wide cognitive perspective, we observed that it was difficult to answer the question, "*How* wide must it be?" This question is answered to some extent when we observe that it is all right to say, "My education was in the sciences/in the humanities," but odd to say, "My education was in biology/in history." In the latter case the cognitive perspective is not wide enough for the activities to be properly termed an "education," and we turn to the concept of "training" which we use to refer to an engagement in *limited* learning and teaching activities. The wider the range of activities, the less specialized they are, the more appropriate it becomes to speak of "education." The narrower and more circumscribed they are, the more appropriate it becomes to speak of "training." (At a certain point "training" merges with "conditioning"—we don't "train" a dog to salivate at the sound of a bell, we "condition" it to do so. We shall analyze what is involved in "conditioning" in a moment.)

With regard to the other two criteria for calling an activity an "educational" activity, it should be observed that a process of "training" *may* satisfy them. Someone who is trained *may* come to care for what he is doing and the activities *may* be intrinsically worthwhile. But there is nothing implied by saying that we have "trained" someone which necessitates that either of these criteria need be satisfied. Certainly there is no implication that training need be in an activity thought to be worthwhile. There is nothing wrong with the notion of "training" someone in the art of torture or hunt-the-thimble. But we might be a little more hesitant about saying that "training" does not imply some sort of caring for the activity in which one has been trained. If a man has been "trained," it seems to imply that he has come to care for certain standards of skill or proficiency. Could we speak of a man as "a trained torturer" if he regularly knocked his victims into a peaceful unconsciousness? Surely a trained torturer is one who cares for certain standards in the refinement of pain, as the trained historian must necessarily care for achieving certain standards of historical scholarship. But this is a rather different sense of "caring" from that which we have previously employed. It is much closer to the notion of "being *careful*" in the exercise of a skill. In this sense, it is possible to "exercise care" in carrying out an activity which one finds distasteful—that is, for which one does not care or think to be worthwhile.

INSTRUCTION

There is *no* sense in which "instruction" implies "caring" on the part of those who have been instructed. There is no parallel here for the notion of a "trained historian" or a "trained torturer." We do not speak of an "instructed historian." When we speak of training someone, we mean not merely that he has learned something, but that he can come up to certain standards of performance in the activity in which he has been trained. Whereas the kind of learning which is implied by the achievement sense of "instruction" is not such that implies that the learner can perform in such a way as to meet certain standards of skill or proficiency. Successful instruction usually implies that the learner has merely imbibed something. Even when instruction is in a skill, such as instruction in driving, successful instruction is evidenced merely by the learner being able to drive—whereas when we speak of a *trained* driver we mean that he is proficient or skillful at driving. And this implies a certain kind of "caring" for the activity—the rather peculiar kind of "caring" which was described a moment ago. But the learning which is produced as a result of successful instruction need not be of a quality that suggests any kind of "caring." If we have received instruction in history or in throwing a ball, and the instruction has been successful, it means that we have understood certain principles which enable us to do history or to throw a ball. But we may carry out these activities in an unskilled way, and this could not be the case if we were "trained historians" or "trained ball throwers."

Nevertheless, although "instruction" implies less than "training" with regard to the care manifested in the performance of the activity, we *may* instruct someone in something in such a way that it is seen to have a wide cognitive perspective. Whereas "training" implies that the activity is circumscribed or specialized or limited in its cognitive range. The fact that the content of "instruction" need not be limited in the way that of "training" is, is bound up with the fact that "instruction" implies that there will be a lot of *telling;* whereas "training" may be carried out by imitation and practice, "instruction" implies that someone is told about the principles involved. We may get someone to imitate us and to practice in the course of instructing him, but this is not, strictly, part of the "instruction." Certainly, driving instructors get their pupils to practice and to imitate certain moves. But when the driving instructor stops *telling* us to release the handbrake as we depress the accelerator when starting on a hill and gets us to *practice* the move, he is changing his teaching method from "instruction" to something else. Isn't it more like "training" then?

"Instruction" has been widely criticized as a teaching method over the last forty or fifty years, particularly in America. There was undoubtedly a need for such criticism of the dominance of "chalk and talk," and we are not likely to be impressed by the concept of education as instruction which the Hadow Report of 1931 referred to as "knowledge to be acquired and facts to be stored." It might seem that "instruction" should be criticized because the knowledge passed on is "knowledge" based only on the authority of the teacher and not "knowledge" appropriately justified to the learner by proofs, evidence, arguments and so on—or so many of the "progressive" educators of the thirties and forties would have us believe. But this is merely poor instruction. There is no reason why proofs and evidence cannot be transmitted through instruction just as easily as the conclusions or facts which they support. So long as there is something statable to be imparted, it can be made part of the content of instruction. In general, however, instruction needs to be supplemented by the sort of practice characteristic of training. If the learner is to gain mastery of the skills in which he is instructed we generally need to supplement the instruction with opportunities for him to apply the knowledge which is imparted.

"Conditioning" is of interest not because it is a technique which is frequently employed in classrooms but because it is a peripheral case of "teaching." An analysis of "conditioning" is essential because it helps us to delimit the edges of the concept of "teaching."

"Conditioning" may be seen to have a "strong" and a "weak" sense. This distinction is a crucial one because in its "weak" sense, "conditioning" may be regarded as coming within the family of concepts headed "teaching." Whereas in its "strong" sense it cannot be classified as a case of "teaching." When we look at "strong" or "strict" conditioning processes we become reluctant to say that the subject could be said to be "learning." We have already argued that the only necessary condition which an activity must satisfy if it is a case of "teaching" is that the pupils *learn* something of what the teacher intends them to learn. The question which comes up in extreme cases of conditioning is whether or not the subjects could properly be said to *learn* anything. Certainly there is an attempt to get the subject to respond in certain ways—a change in behavior of some sort is a necessary condition of successful conditioning. But it is questionable whether or not the behavioral changes are always properly described as evidence of "learning."

The prototype of "strong" conditioning is found in Pavlov's experiments where responses such as salivation were produced in dogs by stimuli such as the sounding of a bell. Pavlov's procedure was, roughly, to continually associate a stimulus such as the bell sounding with the dog's salivatory response to food until the sound of the bell alone was sufficient to produce salivation. This is usually referred to by psychologists as "classical" conditioning. It will be plain, however, that the "weak" sense of conditioning has a much looser connotation than what psychologists call "operant" conditioning.

In its "weak" sense conditioning is a term used rather loosely to refer in a more or less pejorative way to teaching by such techniques as drill and repetition. Thus, for example, we might have walked past a classroom before the advent of the new mathematics teaching where the children were chanting their multiplication tables and heard a comment to the effect that such teaching is really conditioning. Or if we had wandered around the corridors of a school in Nazi Germany and all the children barked "Heil!" whenever we raised our right arm, we might disparagingly say that they had been conditioned. In fact Peter Sellers made a sinister joke by playing on the two senses of "conditioning" in the film *Dr. Strangelove.* One of his roles in the film was the maniac German scientist Dr. Strangelove who advises the U.S. President to atom bomb Russia. Every now and then, in response to "fascist" stimuli such as a sudden command or an authoritarian speaker, his arm would begin to shoot up in the Nazi salute. At which he would struggle with his other arm to restrain his conditioned response, even going so far as to bite and gnaw at the offending arm. The joke, of course, is based on exaggeration for it is extremely rare to build in a response as powerful as this outside the laboratory. It may thus be amusing to imagine what it would be like if what we sometimes speak of loosely as "conditioning" actually had the results produced by conditioning in its strong form. The oddness is created by confusing the two senses of conditioning.

There is surely something very peculiar about saying that conditioning in its strong sense produces learning. Can the dog be said to have learned to salivate at the sound of a bell, or the mad German scientist be said to have learned his uncontrollable reflex if neither can help doing what he does? Could either of them be said to "know how" to carry out these performances? And if they cannot be said to "know how" to carry them out, can they be 'said to have "learned how" to perform in these ways? There is surely something very odd indeed about speaking of "learning" on such occasions. We have no hesitations about saying that a dog "learns" to jump through a hoop or to round up sheep, because the dog has a degree of control over such behavior—they are not merely reflex responses. Similarly we have no hesitation about saying that a child "learns" to say the multiplication tables even if all he can do is chant them. The confusion arises from the fact that the term "conditioning" is sometimes used to refer to cases which clearly involve learning as well as to more questionable cases.

There has been confusion on a grand scale. It is precisely "conditioning" in its strong sense that many learning theorists take as paradigm or classic cases of learning, and learning theory has had widespread influence on the formation of teaching methods. Hull, for example, maintains that there is "no essential distinction between (1) simple associative or trial and error learning and (2) conditioned reflex learning."[5] Hull maintains that the former works in basically the same way as the latter—"responses" are stamped in or "reinforced" in both forms of conditioning. Hull denies the significance of the distinction which is often drawn between "classical" or "strict" conditioning (concerned with reflex responses such as salivation, pupil dilation etc.) and "operant" or "instrumental" conditioning (concerned with movements which are not reflexes, like jumping, bar-pressing etc.). Although Hull's experiments are of the latter sort, this does not constitute, for Hull, an alteration of the model of the learning process provided by classical, Pavlovian conditioning. Although the movements that the subject makes (such as leaping a barrier to avoid an electric shock or pressing a bar to get food from a dispenser) are not reflex responses, neither are they held to be related to the subject's judgment or control in a way that would lead us to speak of them as "actions" rather than as movements. (This is in line with Vesey's remark that in neither "classical" nor "operant" conditioning does the subject recognize either that, or how, its response is instrumental in its obtaining the "reward" or avoiding "punishment." "Insofar as the subject does recognize these things, more is involved than simply its being conditioned."[6]

From these brief references to a highly complex subject we find that some learning theorists seem to be denying themselves

[5] Clark Hull, *Essentials of Behavior* (New Haven: Yale University Press, 1951) p. 16.
[6] G. Vesey, "Conditioning and Learning," *The Concept of Education*, p. 71.

the right to speak of "learning." In their preoccupation with conditioning, the theorists attempt to rule out the very feature of their experiments which might lead us to say that the subject is "learning." They rule out any consideration of the subject's "control" over what it does, any consideration of its acting intelligently in relation to the recognition that its response is instrumental to achieving the "reward" or avoiding the "punishment." Of course, such "mental acts" of "judgment" are not directly observable, but it seems that they are part of what is involved when we distinguish "learning" from merely "developing patterns of response."

INDOCTRINATION

In the film *The Ipcress File* there is a "brainwashing" sequence in which the hero, having been starved and beaten to the limits of his endurance, is put into a large circular container and subjected to a "brain-scrambling" process. Projected kaleidoscopic patterns and colors are designed to completely disorient him and to leave him receptive to the implantation of certain beliefs by his indoctrinators. (In fact the hero retains control by concealing a piece of sharp metal in his hand which he squeezes during the "scrambling" process. The pain enables him to avoid succumbing.)

If the brain-scrambling process permitted the indoctrinator to completely sidestep the independent judgment of the subject and simply induced the subject to respond with specific answers to specific questions, it would surely be more appropriate to refer to this as "conditioning" rather than "indoctrination." "Indoctrination" refers to the alteration of people's beliefs, "conditioning" to the altering of behavior. If the process just described resulted in the hero making quite mechanical verbal responses to stimulus questions, then it could not be said to have anything to do with the alteration of beliefs. We cannot be said to *believe* something unless we can to some extent *understand* it. After hypnosis we may leap to our feet at the hypnotist's signal and say the Apostles' Creed. One could not be said to believe what he professed merely on the grounds that he had recited the words. And for "indoctrination" there has to be the instillation of certain sorts of beliefs.

The implication is that no form of "indoctrination" falls outside the concept of "teaching" because in all cases of successful indoctrination the subject will have "learned" something. (Whereas "strict" or "classical" conditioning, we saw, involves the production of behaviors which it seems odd to say have been "learned.")

So far we have been concerned mainly with tracing the relations and distinctions among each of the members of the family of teaching concepts and to point out the importance of getting these relations and distinctions right. When referring to "indoctrination" it is particularly important that we make clear the relevance of our analysis to what goes on in classrooms. The question which we shall be concerned with is, "To what extent can teachers of history, literary criticism, science and so on be accused of indoctrinating their students?" In order to answer this question it is essential to make a distinction between two senses of "indoctrination." We may distinguish between a "doctrinal" and a "nondoctrinal" sense of "indoctrination." In its "doctrinal" sense, "indoctrination" is distinguished by the nature of its *content*. It refers to the passing on of a body or set of beliefs which rest on assumptions which are either false or for which no publicly acceptable evidence is or can be provided. Possible candidates for "indoctrination" in this sense are the teaching of such economic and political doctrines as Marxism-Leninism or religious doctrines such as Mormonism or Catholicism. In this doctrinal sense, the indoctrinating *methods* may be rational and evidence-regarding—except for the way the basic assumptions of the doctrine are handled. And, further, an indoctrinator in this sense may not be aware that he is indoctrinating.

Much of the difficulty with the concept of indoctrination stems from the existence of other uses of the term which will be called "nondoctrinal" senses of "indoctrination." This nomenclature is designed to emphasize the peculiarity of such uses. There is a degree of logical oddity in claiming that something is a case of "indoctrination" if it does not involve the passing on of a doctrine. Nevertheless, it has been maintained by some philosophers that "indoctrination" can refer to the passing on, as true, of isolated beliefs which are false or questionable (rather than that which is implied by speaking of a "doctrine" i.e., a body or set of beliefs which is false or questionable). An example would be, perhaps, teaching a class of children that the various species of animal life on earth have not passed through a process of evolutionary development, but have always been in the forms that are observable today. In our view, this could only be described as "indoctrination" if it were associated with a whole set of other beliefs which were also being passed on—perhaps a literal Biblical account of the Creation and the many beliefs with which this would be associated. If, however, the teacher is teaching it as an *isolated* belief then he cannot properly be said to be "indoctrinating." If he teaches it as true while knowing it to be false, he is deceiving or lying, but not "indoctrinating." If he does not *know* it is false (and does not associate it with a set of related beliefs) it is a straightforward case of being in error and teaching an error, not a case of "indoctrination."

J. P. White[7] tries to make a case for saying that teaching a boy such falsehoods as "Melbourne is the capital of Australia" or "Uranus has seven moons" could constitute "indoctrination," even if these beliefs were not part of some fantastic doctrine. (They are so "nondoctrinal" that it is very hard to think of a doctrine of which they might be part.) There is some inclination to think there might be something to be said for White's line of thought despite its initial implausibility. It does seem, at first, that if you use certain methods, it is pointless to deny that you are indoctrinating. Let us take a possible way of teaching introductory geology at a university, which largely involves classifying the different rocks according to their chemical composition, hardness, luster, texture, crystal structure, etc. If you get out the rubber truncheons, dazzling white lights and thumbscrews and bludgeon and torture the students into repeating these classifications, are you indoctrinating them? In the case which J. P. White offers, if you go to great lengths to keep the

---

[7] "Indoctrination," *The Concept of Education*, pp. 184–85.

child from finding out that Canberra is the capital of Australia, by keeping him away from Australians, surrounding him with others who are in on the plot to get the boy to hold the belief unshakeably and so on, the argument is that such methods define the process as "indoctrination." The fact that the nature of the methods cannot constitute a sufficient condition for indoctrination is revealed in the case where true geological beliefs are being passed on by "indoctrinatory" methods. True beliefs can, in general, be passed on much more effectively by rational means, and it would ordinarily be just foolish and unnecessary to resort to "indoctrinatory" techniques. We want to say that it is stupid or bizarre teaching rather than "indoctrination." (Philosophers such as White who are concerned simply with what is *conceivable* are seeking to discover logical connections of a very tight sort. We are not denying that someone might claim that our geology teacher is indoctrinating. We are simply pointing out that no one but a philosopher would have got past saying that this procedure is idiotic.) For it only becomes necessary to lay on the truncheon and go in for elaborate deceit when there is likely to be some resistance on the part of the subject to what you're going to teach. And who is going to grit his teeth and hold fast against being persuaded that diamonds have a hardness of ten on a one-to-ten hardness scale, have brilliant luster and are composed of carbon?

Up to this point we have attempted to make plain the peculiarity of speaking of "indoctrination" when referring to the implanting of isolated beliefs, whether true or false. It would seem that only when we are referring to the passing on of a doctrine can we speak of "indoctrination" without oddness. We have equated a doctrine with a body or set of beliefs which rest on assumptions which are either false or which cannot be publicly shown to be true. This account conflicts with the dictionary's first meaning of a "doctrine" as simply, "What is taught." In general, however, what is taught in science, history, literary criticism and so on is not a doctrine. These disciplines are concerned with establishing what is or is not the case about the physical world, the past or about literature. The heliocentric theory of the solar system, for example, is not a doctrine, nor is it part of a doctrine. It is an account of what is the case and is the result of applying the tests and procedures of a form of knowledge, in this case, the physical sciences. There is a fundamental distinction between doctrines on the one hand and on the other, bodies of knowledge which are built up by employing the tests and procedures of such disciplines as science and history.

The second meaning which the dictionary offers is more appropriate—"The teachings of a person or school or church, a particular dogma or tenet." Accordingly, a doctrine is not a set of beliefs which are *publicly* testable, but rather the beliefs of a restricted number of people, the restriction being a necessary consequence of the inability of those who hold the beliefs to publicly demonstrate their truth. Doctrines are thus quite distinct from bodies of knowledge which are built up in such disciplines as science and history, for the tests which such disciplines employ to establish what is or is not the case are not private or personal but are open to public scrutiny.

When we teach children we may legitimately be worried that we are indoctrinating if we are passing on beliefs which we are unable to demonstrate as true. If we are passing on true beliefs, the evidence for which we possess, but which we do not supply to the children, we are still not vulnerable to the accusation that we are indoctrinating. Teaching nonevidentially need not be indoctrination. For example, if we were to teach children that the three angles of a triangle add up to 180°, but we do not provide them with the evidence for this, we are not "indoctrinating." Neither, of course, are we "educating." What we're doing is "telling" or "instructing." A more difficult case is the teaching of moral rules to young children, and this will be the subject of a later chapter. The main difficulty here with regard to indoctrination is that of publicly validating the truth of moral rules. But insofar as we can validate the rules, it would no more be a case of indoctrination to pass on moral rules to children without supplying the evidence for their truth than it is to teach them that the three angles of a triangle add up to 180° without letting them see the evidence.

The clearest cases where we have good reasons for being

worried about indoctrinating are when we are passing on such doctrines as Marxism or Catholicism or Mormonism—if we are trying to convince children that such doctrines are true. We are not concerned here to maintain that these doctrines are false, but much of the evidence for their alleged truth is inaccessible to many people—it is not publicly available. Insofar as this is so, such doctrines are not bodies of *knowledge*, which are the product of the application of public procedures for assessing evidence. Instead, they must be characterized as sets of *beliefs*. Our opposition is not directed against the holding of such beliefs, only against those teachers who attempt to convince children that such beliefs are true when they are unable to provide publicly acceptable evidence for their truth. All that is meant here by "publicly acceptable" is that anyone who tests the evidence will come to the same conclusion. For example, *anyone* who heats metal will find that it expands, *anyone* who examines the history of the French Revolution finds that the peasants played an important part, *anyone* who studies paleontology finds evidence of evolution. But not anyone who examines the evidence for religious beliefs or politico-economic beliefs such as those associated with historical determinism and the class struggle will come to the same conclusion. When the Marxist not merely detects the operation of economic forces in all social change but also claims to be able to see that such forces are invariably the fundamental forces, he is asserting something which is accessible only to initiates. This is a grass roots assumption, and the fact that it cannot be shown to be true makes the chain of argument which follows from it a doctrine rather than a body of knowledge. Anyone who teaches it as true is indoctrinating.

In general, the teaching of such a doctrine will be rational and evidence-regarding, and most of the time it may seem to satisfy the criteria for calling an activity an "educational" activity. For there is a wide cognitive perspective in such doctrines. In a number of respects they may be held to be intrinsically valuable on the grounds that they are, in some respects, developing understanding, and manifestly people come to care very deeply for them. Scheffler fails to take into account the complexity of such doctrines when he holds that indoctrination necessarily fails to involve the independent judgment of the student.[8] For if we were to look in on the teaching of an intelligent Catholic or intelligent Marxist, it would rarely give the appearance of being nonrational. Such doctrines as these are highly rational or coherent edifices erected on foundations which are not open to rational proof. All that the Marxist says about the necessity for the proletariat to gain ownership of the means of production is consistent with and follows from the assumption that economic forces are the fundamental forces in social change. The only point at which the evidence gives out is when the basic assumptions are being passed on. If the teacher is in fact an indoctrinator he will, with regard to certain fundamental assumptions, say, "No, you can't question that" or he will conceal the fact that the basic assumptions are not demonstrably true. If the Marxist is not an indoctrinator he will make it plain, when the fundamental assumption that the economic factors are invariably the basic factors in social change comes up for examination, that this is incapable of demonstration in a number of cases. Of course, what often happens is that in cases where the fundamental factor seems to be the decision of an historical protagonist or the influence of a religious movement, an elaborate story is told to show how the great man's decision or the religious movement is "really" the product of economic circumstances. Or, more bluntly, the teacher may say "You can't question that assumption because Marx held it to be true." We may have heard, too, of teachers of religious doctrines who maintain that everyone has experience of God, and those who deny it are willfully blinding themselves to this experience. It is this introduction of what Professor Hirst[9] has termed a "logical stopper" that makes what is being taught into a doctrine and the teacher into an indoctrinator. Apart from such fundamental questions, the teacher may be prepared to give reasons, promote understanding and so on. But if we chase him back to fundamentals and we find that all his views stem

[8] Scheffler, "Philosophical Models of Teaching," p. 131.
[9] Professor Hirst used this description during a seminar at the University of London Institute of Education in 1967.

from accepting a basic premise without being able to give satisfactory reasons for it, then the whole teaching process must be seen in retrospect as an attempt to indoctrinate. (It is important to note that nothing turns on whether or not the examples which have been taken of indoctrination are good examples. The whole argument could be put in conditional form, i.e., *insofar as* the basic assumptions of a set of beliefs cannot be publicly demonstrated to be true, then teaching them as true is indoctrination.)

If we accept the argument so far we could easily become nervous that what we are teaching in most school subjects might ultimately be judged to be indoctrination. In subjects such as English and history it frequently happens that university students are encouraged (either tacitly or explicitly) to become followers of a "school of thought," i.e., they are encouraged to adopt a particular line of approach to the study of their subject, to the exclusion of other lines of approach. And often the rejection of other possible approaches takes place in advance of seeing what they are really about. This has certainly occurred in the case of the *Scrutiny* school of literary critics which has abstained, on Leavis' advice, from what Leavis called "abstract" philosophizing or theorizing about literary criticism—and this in advance of seeing whether it could get anywhere. If he has been brought up to toe the Leavis line a conscientious teacher could begin to get suspicious about the underlying assumptions of his teaching to the extent that he might wonder if he had himself been indoctrinated and if he was in turn indoctrinating his own pupils. But paradoxically enough this sort of worry is probably a sign that a man has not been indoctrinated. To the extent that Leavisites or Marxists or Catholics intelligently question the assumptions of their masters then to that extent they may have been "educated" rather than "indoctrinated." (At the same time we are not supporting R. M. Hare's extraordinary view[10] that in order for a teacher to avoid indoctrination he must be pleased if his pupils question *everything* he says. This is liberalism running riot!)

[10] R. M. Hare, "Adolescents into Adults," *Aims in Education*, ed. T. H. B. Hollins (Manchester, England: Manchester University Press, 1964) p. 70.

The point is not to decry the existence of "schools of thought" in university departments nor their propagation by schoolteachers. It is not illegitimate, in the business of initiating people into a discipline, that there be a "master" and "disciples." It is a matter of great tact, of course, for the "master" to avoid getting personal allegiance at the expense of passing on the techniques and procedures of thinking which may in the end be used to question what he himself has said (a point which Peters makes somewhere?). But that this is a very important part of education is surely indisputable. Many of the best teachers are those who might most easily be charged with indoctrination. They are teachers who care deeply about a particular approach to a subject, and they pass on the caring as well as the subject. They are, perhaps, the teachers we sometimes say we have "moved beyond." But "moving beyond" one's teacher is often a major step in one's education.

This is certainly not to say that insofar as a teacher is unsuccessful in passing on his approach to his subject that he is to this extent an educator rather than an indoctrinator. Such a position would plainly be absurd and it is connected with Hare's view from which we have already dissociated ourselves. It is quite possible to "move beyond" the views and procedures we have assimilated from a teacher whether he is to be appropriately described as a master of a discipline *or* as an indoctrinator. We *may* have been indoctrinated and yet eventually come to see the limitations and obscurities of the doctrine, just as we may have learned the concepts and procedures of a particular approach to a discipline and yet "move beyond" them. The mere fact that we may eventually question views which have been instilled into us by a process of indoctrination need not mitigate the extent to which the process we underwent was a process of indoctrination. To be sure, "indoctrination" in its "achievement" sense must, logically, be successful. But an indoctrinator may be as realistic about the changes which may take place in a student's views over a period of time and through competing influences as is the educator. It would be misleading to maintain either that success in indoctrination implied that the pupil *never* afterward changed his views or that the educator ought to be other than resigned to the fact that students will often come to reject views and procedures to which he himself is attached.

If we cannot distinguish between education and indoctrination on these grounds, how can we do so? In such subjects as literary criticism, history, sociology and psychology, there are few publicly agreed criteria for making judgments, at least where major concepts and procedures are under examination. As a result we have a proliferation of "schools of thought" in these subjects. How can we distinguish between a doctrine and a discipline here? The Leavisite, the scientific historian, the Freudian psychologist, the Keynesian economist—all may be as convinced of the truth of their basic assumptions as the Marxist or the Catholic, but all will to varying extents run into trouble in attempting to make their truth publicly demonstrable.

The answer to this is far from clear. What we have done is to bring out the problem concealed by our original account of "indoctrination" as the passing on of a system or set of beliefs which are such that at some point they may be seen to rest on assumptions for which no publicly acceptable evidence is or can be provided. The problem comes when we ask who is to adjudicate the truth of the assumptions. Who is to adjudicate the claims of Freudian psychology, Marxist economics, Leavisite criticism or Catholicism to be forms of knowledge? It is tempting to suggest that this sort of second order work is peculiarly that of the philosopher. The fact that he is often treated as a trespassing outsider by insiders who are busy propagating their particular lines may be an indication that the particular line, whatever it is, will not bear a detached analytic scrutiny. It could be that the degree of openness to philosophic searching which is revealed by the proponents of a particular line of enquiry is indicative of the degree to which the line is a doctrine rather than a form of knowledge. On this basis, scientists, historians and mathematicians, for example, come out rather well, since they have each taken very seriously the need for philosophic scrutiny of their logical characteristics and basic assumptions. Whereas literary critics and Freudian psychologists, for example, show a marked resistance to the intrusion of the philosopher into their domains. Typically the reaction of the Freudian psychologist to a questioning of his assumptions is to analyze the motives of the questioner, and the Freudian is prone to suggest that the reason why he wants to question the validity of psychoanalytic theory is a matter of his deepseated unconscious defenses against psychoanalytic probing of his own personality. We will be criticizing this sort of reply in more detail in a later chapter. The main point to note is that it becomes impossible to see what *would* count as a falsification of Freudian assumptions if they are defended in this manner. For any attempt to falsify them leads us into a dead end if such attempts are themselves evidence of Freudian assumptions. Conversely, it is impossible to verify the assumptions. The Freudian could hardly maintain that only those who seek to support his views are mentally healthy and that those who seek to undermine it are disturbed. The fact that this is sometimes what Freudians do seem to be saying is perhaps indicative that theirs is a doctrine rather than a body of knowledge.

Literary criticism, on the other hand, seems neither to be a doctrine nor a form of knowledge. In the next chapter it will be argued that literary criticism and some aspects of historical enquiry employ criteria for making judgments which are not fully statable and thus not fully public. It does not follow, of course, that this makes all teaching of them indoctrination. In order to avoid this accusation, all the teacher has to do is to make clear to his students the areas of uncertainty. The indoctrinator, on the other hand, will either deny that there are uncertainties or try to conceal them in his teaching.

The main point which has been made in this section is that the test of indoctrination is not a matter of the methods employed but a matter of whether the body of beliefs and procedures being passed on are true. The fact that it is often very *difficult* to decide whether or not they are true in no way affects the contention that this is the criterion which we try to operate when we are using the concept of "indoctrination" appropriately. All it does is make it difficult to apply. It has also been argued that to speak of "indoctrination" in isolated beliefs is misleading. If isolated beliefs which are false are taught as if they were true, this is either deception or teaching a mistake. "Indoctrination," on the other hand, involves a systematic attempt to pass on as true a set of beliefs which are basically unfounded.

BASIC READING

DEARDEN, R. F., "Instruction and Learning by Discovery," *The Concept of Education*, R. S. Peters, ed. London: Routledge & Kegan Paul, 1967.

FLEW, A., "What is Indoctrination?" *Studies in Philosophy and Education*, Vol. IV. No. 3, Spring 1966. Obtainable from Southern Illinois University, Edwardsville, Illinois 62025. U.S.A.

HARE, R. M., "Adolescents into Adults," *Aims in Education*, J. H. B. Hollins ed. Manchester, England: Manchester Univ. Press, 1964.

SCHEFFLER, I., *The Language of Education*, Chapters 4 and 5. Illinois: Thomas, 1960.

———, "Philosophical Models of Teaching," *Philosophy and Education*, 2d ed. I. Scheffler, ed. Boston: Allyn and Bacon, Inc., 1966.

VESEY, G., "Conditioning and Learning," *The Concept of Education*.

WHITE, J. P., "Indoctrination," *The Concept of Education*.

WILSON, J., "Education and Indoctrination," *Aims in Education*.

FURTHER REFERENCES

ATKINSON, R. F., "Instruction and Indoctrination," *Philosophical Analysis and Education*, Archambault, R. D., ed. London: Routledge & Kegan Paul, 1965.

GREEN, T. F., "Teaching, Acting and Behaving," *Studies in Philosophy and Education*, III, (Winter, 1964-1965).

OAKESHOTT, M., "Learning and Teaching," *The Concept of Education*.

RYLE, G., "Teaching and Training," *The Concept of Education*.

WILSON, J., "Comment on Flew's 'What is Indoctrination?' " *Studies in Philosophy and Education,* Vol. IV. No. 4, Spring 1966.

DISCUSSION/ESSAY TOPICS

* To what extent (if any) do you find that Peters and Scheffler offer us an ideal of "teaching" rather than an analysis of the concept?

* In what ways may "training" and "instruction" complement one another in an educational process?

* "Every education system makes use of indoctrination. Children are indoctrinated with the multiplication table; they are indoctrinated with love of country; they are indoctrinated with the principles of chemistry and physics and mathematics and biology, and nobody finds fault with indoctrination in these fields. Yet these are of small concern in the great business of life by contrast with ideas concerning God and man's relation to God, his neighbour and himself, man's nature and his supernatural destiny." (Quoted by J. S. Brubacher, *Eclectic Philosophy of Education*).

Discuss.

* Is religious education possible? Or must it all be indoctrination?

3

Knowledge and Education: Logical and Psychological Considerations

(A) THE CONTENT OF EDUCATION

WE HAVE FOUND that if we are to avoid indoctrinating children what we teach as true must *be* true and its truth must be publicly assessable. The public procedures for assessing truth in various fields are to be found in the various forms of knowledge such as science, history, mathematics and so on. We have noticed that in some subjects the nature of the procedures and the criteria according to which some judgments are assessed as true or false are obscure or disputed, and we held that teachers are obliged to make students aware of these areas of uncertainty. This is a difficult task if a teacher has never attempted a philosophic analysis of the nature of his subject and since most teachers have not done so we will spend most of this chapter discussing the nature of a "form of knowledge" with reference to particular subjects.

But first there is a fundamental question which we cannot afford to take for granted. We argued earlier that the activities which compose education are worthwhile in themselves. But we have not, as yet, offered any grounds for saying that such subjects as science, history, literary criticism and so on are worthwhile in themselves.

What did we mean when we said that an educational activity is "worthwhile in itself?" If we were to go up to a man in the street and ask him "What are the worthwhile activities which comprise education?" he would probably choke. But if we persisted he would probably come up with an answer such as "those activities which will fit people for jobs when they leave school." We maintained earlier on that this view was mistaken on two grounds:

(1) The value of the activities which compose education must be capable of a more than merely instrumental justification; i.e., they cannot be merely something that one goes through in order that some desirable outcome will ensue, such as getting a suitable job. Part of what is meant by "education" is that activities which are worthwhile in themselves are being engaged in. Peters overstates the point as follows:

> It would be a logical contradiction to say that a man had been educated but that he had in no way changed for the better, or that in educating his son a man was attempting nothing that was worthwhile. This is a purely conceptual point. Such a connection between "education" and what is valuable does not imply any particular commitment to content. It is a further question what the particular standards are in virtue of which activities are thought to be of value and what grounds there might be for claiming that these are the correct ones.[1]

(2) There is a crucial distinction between "education" and vocational training. While we *may* be educating someone as we train him for a vocation, we need not be. If we were to teach a trainee nurse how to tie a bandage or a trainee truck

[1] Peters, *Ethics and Education*, p. 25. (Peters' "overstatement" is to maintain that there would be a "logical contradiction" involved in claiming that someone had been educated but had not changed for the better. We argued at the conclusion of Chapter 1 that it would be "odd" or "peculiar" to maintain this but that the connection between "education" and engaging in worthwhile activities was not "analytic.")

driver how to change gears we would not be educating them. We are *just* training them. But if we are teaching a potential geologist what "igneous" means or a potential historian what is meant by "Industrial Revolution" there is at least the possibility that we are educating them. For as we shall argue in a moment, teaching someone the concepts which are fundamental to a form of knowledge may be said to be worthwhile in itself; whereas there is nothing *intrinsically* worthwhile in being able to tie a bandage or change gears. The purposes which are thus served may be thought to be extremely worthwhile—being able to tie a bandage correctly may save a life—but there is a clear distinction between the activity itself (tieing the bandage) which is quite valueless, quite worthless, and the end or purpose which it serves.

There need be no distinction between means and ends in learning or teaching geology, history, physics, mathematics and so on. Although these activities *may* serve purposes outside themselves, they are worthwhile in themselves whether they do so or not. Such activities are at least potentially educational activities, whereas activities which are *only* valuable insofar as they are the means to achieving some extrinsic purpose thought to be worthwhile, such as getting a suitable job, logically cannot be educational activities. At most they will be a form of training though they may only be a form of drill.

How would we reply to a practical man who insisted that all this talk of intrinsic value is a philosopher's fantasy and who asserted that education or anything else must be shown to be useful if it is to be valuable? We would have to show him that there is something wrong with holding that everything which is valuable is instrumentally valuable. If he were to claim, for example, that the value of teaching science is that it is the means to providing more trained manpower we could ask him why he thought the provision of more trained manpower to be valuable. If he replied that this is a means to achieving national prosperity we could ask him why he thought *this* to be valuable, and so on, ad infinitum. We would then have to point out to him that it is not admissable for him to continue in this way and that he must at some point hold that something is intrinsically valuable. For the meaning of the term "valuable" is not being defined, but is being lost in an "infinite regress." Our practical man might want to know what is wrong with an infinite regress. We could do no better than to direct him to Bertrand Russell's distinction between two forms of infinite regression; one which does not involve the meaning of the terms involved and another which does, and which is inadmissible or "vicious."

> Wherever the meaning of a proposition is in question, an infinite regress is objectionable, since we never reach a proposition which has a definite meaning.[2]

Thus Peters is able to maintain that

> . . . instrumental or technical judgements derive their normative force [from] judgments about activities or states of affairs which are intrinsically good.[3]

It is one thing to see the distinction between activities which are worthwhile in themselves and activities which are instrumentally valuable. It is quite another thing to see why the development of understanding through the various forms of knowledge is worthwhile in itself. How do we cope with such a radical questioning of this as B. H. Bode's who asks:

> Why should any of the subjects at present studied in the school curriculum be studied at all? The dyed-in-the-wool traditionalist is disposed to treat this question cavalierly. To him, knowledge is worthwhile on its own account. This is apt to be the substance of his reply, somewhat adorned, perhaps, by allusions to "culture", to the joys of intellectual pursuits and to the desirability of cultivating the mind.[4]

What we are proposing to do is to defend the "substance" of the traditionalist's reply. But it is worth noting as well that allusions to "culture," to the joys of intellectual pursuits and to

---

[2] Bertrand Russell, *The Principles of Mathematics* (London: Allen and Unwin Ltd., 1903) p. 349. Russell's remark was pointed out to me by Mr. W. Smith of Melbourne University.

[3] R. S. Peters, *Ethics and Education*, p. 154.

[4] B. H. Bode, *Modern Educational Theories* (New York: Vintage Books, first published 1927) pp. 53–54.

the desirability of cultivating the mind need not be mere adornments of the view that knowledge is worthwhile on its own account. Rather, they reflect the fact that people who engage in the pursuit of knowledge generally come to care for its pursuit. To dismiss such an involvement as Bode does is to adopt an external view of such activities as science, history and mathematics. We are inclined to suggest to someone who speaks as if "the joys of intellectual pursuits" were beyond his understanding that he try *doing* mathematics or science for a while in order to see what is meant. Bode places himself roughly in the position of a child who has never been engaged in a discipline who asks, "Why should I do history rather than play football?" And there is not much more we can say to the child than, "Try doing history, for once you get into it you will come to see what makes it worthwhile."

But such a reply is hardly likely to satisfy Bode (or the child!). So we must change our tack and concentrate on Bode's question, "Why should any of the subjects at present studied in the school curriculum be studied at all?" For the fundamental question is, "How can the pursuit of knowledge be justified?" (For the purposes of this argument such "subjects" as basket-weaving and grammar will be ignored. The argument which follows is concerned only with those subjects which are "forms" or "fields" of knowledge.)

If we think for a moment about Bode's question it begins to seem rather peculiar, for surely Bode shows himself to be committed to some degree to the very pursuit he seems to be questioning. In asking for a justification for the pursuit of knowledge he is surely revealing that he is engaged in just that pursuit. Asking for justifications is precisely the sort of activity which is basic to the pursuit of knowledge in all its forms. Scientific, literary, critical, geographical theories are worth nothing if no justification for their being held can be put forward. The particular form of knowledge in which Bode reveals himself to be already involved is philosophy and the point which he has already reached is a limiting question in philosophy: there can be no way of asking "Why pursue truth?" without at the same time showing yourself to be already in its pursuit. As Hirst puts it,

> To question the pursuit of any kind of rational knowledge is in the end self-defeating, for the questioning itself depends on accepting the very principles whose use is finally being called in question.[5]

Furthermore, Bode must care about the pursuit of truth, too, at least to the extent that he thinks it is worth asking this question. Of course such minimal engagement is a long way from "the joys of intellectual pursuits," but as with the child whose view of the pursuit of truth is an external one, we cannot expect a high degree of caring unless the questioner is on the inside of a form of knowledge.

The importance of being "on the inside" of a form of knowledge in order to grasp the notion of what is intrinsically worthwhile in this context can hardly be overestimated. Part of what is involved in getting "on the inside" is the discovering that there are standards for performance which are built into any activity which is a form of knowledge. It is unlikely that many would be deeply persuaded that the pursuit of knowledge was intrinsically worthwhile by the foregoing argument that to question the pursuit of knowledge is to reveal a degree of commitment to the pursuit. But obviously one's grasp of what is meant by the intrinsic value of seeking knowledge must be largely dependent on one's grasp of the standards which are built into particular forms of knowledge.

It follows from this argument that inquiries into the "aims" of teaching a subject which merely look outward to the achievement of extrinsic ends thought to be valuable miss a crucial characteristic of activities such as science and history—that immanent in them are those principles of rational inquiry without which questions about "ends" or "justification" would be meaningless. To cite Hirst again,

[5] P. H. Hirst, "Liberal Education and the Nature of Knowledge," *Philosophical Analysis and Education,* ed. R. D. Archambault (London: Routledge and Kegan Paul, Ltd., 1965) p. 127. Reprinted by permission of Routledge and Kegan Paul, Ltd. and Humanities Press, Inc.

> Justification is only possible if what is being justified is both intelligible under publicly rooted concepts and is assessable according to accepted criteria. It assumes commitment to these two principles. But these principles are in fact fundamental to the pursuit of knowledge in all its forms. . . . The forms of knowledge are in a sense simply the working out of these general principles in particular ways.[6]

If the development of mind through knowledge is seen to be, in this sense, intrinsically valuable, an exploration of the "aims" of teaching a subject must be largely unnecessary if what is being sought is extrinsic to the pursuit of knowledge, for,

> . . . to acquire knowledge is to become aware of experience as structured, organized and made meaningful in some quite specific way, and the varieties of human knowledge constitute the highly developed forms in which man has found this possible. To acquire knowledge is to learn to see, to experience the world in a way otherwise unknown, and thereby to have a mind in a fuller sense. . . . To have a mind basically involves coming to have experience articulated by means of various conceptual schema. It is only because man has over millennia objectified and progressively developed these that he has achieved the forms of human knowledge, and the possibility of the development of mind as we know it is open to us today.[7]

It follows that when we do what is usually called "method" work in our subject in a college or school of education the customary work on finding out what are the "aims" of teaching the subject ought to be replaced by a consideration of the way the subject may structure, organize and make meaningful the experience of children in quite specific ways. Or, rather, this *is* the appropriate way to specify what the aims are, for the aims are intrinsic to the activity of pursuing knowledge and thus to the development of mind.

In many cases, those of us who are engaged in such method work have already achieved a degree of mastery of our subject which is such that we could claim to be "on the inside"

[6] Ibid., p. 126.
[7] Ibid., pp. 124–25.

of the particular form or field of knowledge. Most of our previous teaching will have been designed to immerse us in the
concepts and procedures of the subject largely by practice and
discussion with those who are already on the inside. Our experience will already have been structured and organized in
highly specific ways but we are nevertheless unlikely to be able
to describe the logical characteristics of this structure and
organization. To employ Hirst's terms, we are unlikely to be
able to give an adequate account of the following characteristics of our subject:

(1) The nature of the key concepts which are distinctive of
the subject.

(2) The characteristic relations between the key concepts.

(3) The criteria according to which judgments are assessed
for truth or falsity within the subject.

In brief, we may have little detachment of a philosophic or
second order kind from our subject. And since no consideration
of the way a subject may structure and organize the experience
of children can even begin until the structure and organization
of the subject itself is examined, it follows that philosophical
analysis of a subject is the prior task in method classes. Instead
of having our eyes turned outward towards extrinsic aims we
ought to be turning them back onto our subject with a detached and analytic gaze.

(B) FORMAL LOGIC AND THE LOGIC OF A FORM OF KNOWLEDGE

We have promised to clarify what is meant by the logical characteristics of a form of knowledge by referring more specifically to particular subjects. But no philosopher would permit
himself to do this until he had distinguished what he meant by
"logic" in this context from formal logic.

The laws of formal logic, as Strawson points out, are laws
which "are not confined to discussion of any one particular
kind of subject but may be found to occur in discussions of
utterly heterogeneous topics." They are "rules such that the
knowledge that any one of them had been broken in a certain

piece of discourse gives no clue as to what that piece of discourse is about."[8] A law of formal logic, such as the principle of noncontradiction, is not relevant to what people do when they attempt to establish a claim to know something. It is rather a principle the observance of which is essential if the attempt is to be intelligible. As Toulmin points out, we must eliminate inconsistencies and self-contradictions before we shall have expressed ourselves in an intelligible manner, for "consistency and coherence are prerequisites for rational assessment." Toulmin's account of the way formal logical laws function is the clearest statement of the matter available:

> A man who purports to make an assertion, but who contradicts himself in doing so, will fail even to make himself understood. The question whether what he says is true cannot even be reached. So also, a man who puts forward a series of statements in an argument but whose final conclusion contradicts certain of his data, [i.e. his premisses] fails to make himself understood; until his case is stated in consistent, coherent form, questions about the merit of the conclusion or argument cannot yet be asked. Self-contradictory statements and conclusions inconsistent with our data, are ones which have to be ruled out before we can even get a case stated clearly or in proper form: this incoherence is accordingly a preliminary matter, which compels us to debar them at the very outset.[9]

So that when we object to an argument on the grounds that it breaks a law of formal logic, e.g., the conclusion contradicts the premises, we are not concerned with the particular claim to know something, but simply with understanding what is being said. For example, if someone were to maintain that all swans are black and then to refer to a white bird as a swan we would not start a survey of the color of swans to find out what was wrong with what he is saying. For his self-contradiction makes what he says unintelligible.

[8] P. F. Strawson, *Introduction to Logical Theory* (London: Methuen and Co., Ltd.; New York: John Wiley & Sons, Inc., 1952) pp. 40–41.

[9] Stephen Toulmin, *The Uses of Argument* (Cambridge, England: Cambridge University Press, 1958) p. 29.

Whereas the laws of formal logic are those principles which must be observed if a claim to know something is to be intelligible, the logic of a form of knowledge refers to the principles which decide whether or not particular intelligible claims to know something are true or false. The logical characteristics of each form of knowledge are distinct from one another. That is to say, each form of knowledge exhibits distinct concepts, distinctive relations between the concepts and distinctive criteria for judging whether an assertion is valid or invalid. Since this abstract talk may be hard to follow we will be as specific as possible and attempt to bring out the logical distinctness of certain areas of knowledge. A convenient way of doing this is to examine the current debate between those philosophers of history who would assimilate historical arguments to a scientific or quasi-scientific model and those who defend its logical distinctness on the grounds that historical *concepts* are distinct and that therefore the procedures for defining the relations between them and for arriving at historical judgments must be logically distinctive.

The historian's procedure is typically the weighing and balancing of evidence; but some historians and philosophers of history think that this is not good enough. They argue that the weighing and balancing of evidence should be replaced, at least when the historian is questioned about his judgment by deduction from empirically validated laws, if their conclusions are to be rationally acceptable. These historians, often referred to as "covering law theorists," are advocating what is often called "scientific history." Just as many scientific judgments are validated by reference to a covering empirical law, such as "all swans are white" or "all diamonds have a hardness of ten on a one-to-ten hardness scale" or "all tidal movements are caused by the moon"; so it is argued that historians must turn to comparable laws to validate their judgments. The two clearest exponents of the cases for and against this are P. Gardner, a covering law theorist who wrote *The Nature of Historical Explanation* and W. Dray who wrote *Laws and Explanation in History*. Dray's main argument is that an historical explanation specifies events and states of affairs which are in an important sense *unique,* and that it would therefore be pointless to look for a covering empirical generalization. The issue becomes initially a matter of asking, "What is the nature of the concepts with which the historian deals? Are historical events and states of affairs unique in an important sense?"

In one sense they are not unique. Gardner points out that historians classify events and things as falling into types or kinds, as may be seen in their use of general terms like "revolution" and "conquest." So far as it goes, Gardner's is an appropriate *kind* of argument for suggesting that certain kinds of concepts are involved in a judgment. Gardner goes on to imply that the kind of judgment entailed by this understanding of the nature of historical concepts will be the bringing of historical events under "laws."

Dray meets this argument by pointing out that "historical events and conditions are often unique simply in the sense of being different from others with which it would be natural to group them under a classification term."[10] Dray suggests that if the historian were to use his classificatory terms correctly, he would be more concerned with the *differences* between the cases within the classification than with the classification itself.

> It is my contention that the historian, when he sets out to explain the French Revolution is just not interested in explaining it as *a* Revolution—as an astronomer might be interested in explaining a certain eclipse as an instance of eclipses; he is almost invariably concerned with it as different from other members of its class.[11]

Dray adds that the uniqueness of the historical event, despite the classificatory terms used to refer to it, is to be seen by comparing the generality of the naturalist's expression, "the whale," with the particularity of the historian's "the French Revolution." And Dray turns immediately from his analysis of the nature of historical concepts to the distinctive logic of the

---

[10] W. H. Dray, *Laws and Explanation in History* (Oxford: The Clarendon Press, 1957) p. 47. By permission of the Clarendon Press.
[11] Ibid.

procedures necessary to establish judgments in this form of knowledge. If he is right about the uniqueness of the concepts, as he seems to be, it would be pointless to look for covering laws—"the notion of a generalization with but a single case would ordinarily be regarded as a self-contradictory one."[12]

Events and situations of the past are not the only kinds of concepts that the historian attempts to relate, of course. Historians are commonly concerned with the motives and purposes of historical characters. Is it possible to identify procedures for moving among and relating such concepts in historical discourse which are logically distinct from scientific procedures? Some covering law theorists maintain that any historical explanation in terms of motives, purposes and so on depends for its validity on covert appeals to psychological laws. Even Popper, who rejects the view that history is a "generalizing science" (such as physics, biology, sociology, etc.) argues that

> . . . if we explain Caeser's decision to cross the Rubicon by his ambition and energy, say, then we are using some very trivial psychological generalizations which would hardly ever arouse the attention of a psychologist.[13]

But Popper uses the term "generalization" interchangeably with the term "law," and Dray points out that "generalizations" are very different from "laws." It is a mistake to argue, as Popper does, that the sort of generalization to which he refers is just a very loose scientific law. Again the model of scientific explanation is inappropriate to historical explanation. The "psychological generalization" in Popper's example would probably be something like, "Ambition and energy make men take on big tasks." It would not only be trivial, it would not function as a warrant for an historical judgment. The trivial generalization may well be something which the historian has in mind when he looks for an explanation of why Caesar crossed the Rubicon, but the validity of the "psychological generalization" is not his

---

[12] Ibid., p. 40.
[13] K. R. Popper, *The Open Society and its Enemies* (London: Routledge and Kegan Paul, Ltd., 1962) vol. 2, p. 265.

concern (*qua* historian) at all. He examines the historical
evidence—Caesar's speeches, comments of contemporaries,
etc.—to find out if it appears that Caesar was motivated in this
or some other way. The historian is concerned with whether, in
this particular case, energy and ambition were important factors. He must make a distinct kind of judgment, involving the
weighing and balancing of evidence, not a rather vague and
inadequate subsumption under a trivial generalization.

Something of the diversity of the procedures by which the
historian moves towards an historical judgment, and the cor-
responding flexibility of the criteria by which his judgments
are measured is revealed by Dray's account of the various ways
it is both necessary and legitimate for the historian to assess
the motives and intentions of historical agents. Thus, for example, he recognizes the point of "empathy" in historical explanation, "for we build up to an explanatory equilibrium *from
the evidence.*"

> To get inside Disraeli's shoes the historian does not simply
> ask himself, "What would I have done?" He reads Disraeli's
> dispatches, his letters, his speeches etc.—and not with the
> purpose of discovering antecedent conditions falling under
> some empirically validated law, but rather in the hope of
> appreciating the problem as Disraeli saw it.[14]

Dray's claim that this is an appropriate procedure for establishing certain kinds of historical judgments is obviously not dependent on any notion of imaginative "leaps." It is a calculation from the evidence. By such means, suggests Dray, we can
display the "rationale" of an historical agent's actions. And
further,

> The goal of such explanation is to show that what was done
> was the thing to have done for the reasons given, rather
> than merely the thing that is done on such occasions, per-
> haps in accordance with certain laws (loose or otherwise)
> . . . there is an element of *appraisal* of what was done in
> such explanations, . . . what we want to know when we

[14] Dray, *Laws and Explanation in History,* p. 126.

have the action explained is in what way it was appropriate.[15]

To record what the agent *said* his reasons were would
not be enough to provide rational explanation unless the
cogency of such reported reasons could be appreciated by
the historian, when any particular beliefs, purposes, or principles of the agent were taken into account. . . . The historian must be able to "work" the agent's calculation.[16]

It will perhaps be argued that if this is what the so-called
"logic" of history amounts to, then it cannot be maintained that
the judgments which are formed could be claims to *know* that
something is the case—that this is not, at times, a description
of the logic of a form of knowledge. In many historical ex-
planations this could become a genuine doubt. It certainly is
a genuine doubt about many judgments made by literary critics
as well. In fact some distinguished literary critics customarily
deny themselves a claim to knowledge. They put their judgments in the form of questions, "This is the case, isn't it?" The
concepts and procedures which characterize literary critical
arguments are elusive and unstable in a way often similar to
some historical concepts and procedures. And yet literary critics
and historians carry on their arguments without using criteria
which are "public" in the sense of always being statable. In the
case of literary criticism this must be partly attributed to the
lack of second-order work on the nature of this discipline. The
relations between literary critical concepts and the nature of
the criteria for testing the truth or falsity of judgments in this
domain are sometimes not statable only because no one has
made a concerted attempt to state them. The philosophy of
literary criticism is a sadly neglected area. If we do begin to
explain the relations between such concepts as "imagery,"
"movement," "rhythm" and so on in the work of literary critics,
or the nature of the criteria implied by such a concept as "real-
ization," it becomes apparent that the "logic" of this discipline
is highly flexible and often "subjective" because it lacks clearly
specifiable public criteria for making judgments. In such cases

[15] Ibid., p. 124.
[16] Ibid., p. 126.

there are certainly relationships which approximate in varying degrees the logical relations discernible in a form of knowledge, but it seems more appropriate to refer to them as exhibiting the "logic of a form of discourse."

It should be obvious from our cursory examination of the "logic" of history that there is nothing "final" about the organization of forms of knowledge. The fact that there is debate among those who are on the inside of a particular form of knowledge reflects this clearly. A teacher of any subject which is a form of knowledge is severely handicapped if he is unable to take a "second order" or philosophical view of the logic of his subject, especially if it is being debated. Such a teacher runs the formidable risk of teaching many things which are actually uncertain as if they were true.

The other point which emerges from our analysis of the logical characteristics of history is the considerable complexity of its structure and organization. And the subject teacher's fundamental concern to identify the specific ways in which a subject can structure, organize and make meaningful the experience of children cannot even begin until the structure and organization of the subject itself is examined.

(C) KNOWLEDGE AND ABILITY

We have maintained that education is concerned with the development of mind through knowledge, and we have specified to some extent what is meant by "knowledge." But there are serious misconceptions in some educational circles about the nature of knowledge which need special attention. The most dangerous misconception at present is about the relationship between "knowledge" and "ability." In this section we will expose this misconception in the work of a curriculum theorist, and in the following section we will try to dig out the philosophical roots of the misconception.

One of the most influential books in curriculum theory at present is *A Taxonomy of Educational Objectives*, by B. S. Bloom and his colleagues. In this book we find that educational objectives are divided into two main categories—"knowledge" and "skills and abilities."[17] Bloom refers to knowledge as entirely a matter of *remembering* or *recalling* facts, principles, methods and so on. The so-called "ability" to "comprehend" is not necessary to knowledge nor is it a relevant consideration in testing for knowledge. "Knowledge" to Bloom and his colleagues is entirely a matter of what can be remembered; comprehending, applying, analyzing are skills or abilities which are not essential to *knowing*. Knowing is entirely what you can parrot off; it is essentially mindless.

The point is that the ability to parrot off information is by no means a sufficient condition for knowing something. We cannot say that even the simplest kinds of information such as "London is the capital of England" are *known* until they are *understood*. And the way to test whether such a fact is known is to test for the "abilities" which Bloom and company quite falsely separate from knowledge. To the extent to which a man does not comprehend, could not apply, or could not analyze his proposition that "London is the capital of England," then to that extent he cannot be said to *know* that London is the capital of England. For these are tests for having the *concept* of "England" and of "London" and of being able to relate them by the concept of a capital.

But perhaps it seems odd to say that a man must be able to *apply* his knowledge, for example, in order for us to say that he has the knowledge. If so, consider the following example. We have a man who has passed a number of tests for comprehending the proposition that "London is the capital of England." Thus, when he was asked to point out the capital of England on a blank map, he wrote "London" in the appropriate place; we put him in Leicester and told him to head for the capital, and he went off in the right direction down the M. 1. Highway to London. But then we found that he just could not grasp the fact that Canberra is the capital of Australia. Instead, he kept saying that Sydney must be the capital. We might start to wonder if his concept of a capital was "the largest city in a

[17] See, for example, the Condensed Taxonomy, pp. 201–07, *A Taxonomy of Educational Objectives,* B. S. Bloom, et al. (London: Longmans, Green & Co., Ltd., 1964).

country." And would we not also wonder if his failure meant that he did no really *know* that London is the capital of England?

This illustration suggests that all the so-called mental abilities and skills are part of what is involved in knowing something. For *knowing* something involves judging that something is so, and judgment is a complex mental operation. Mental abilities and skills are not separable from knowing something, for we are unable to *specify* or *describe* mental abilities and skills independently of the various forms of knowledge. In order to attribute a mental ability or skill to someone, we have to be able to say that his performance comes up to certain standards, satisfies certain criteria. And these standards, these criteria, are logical ones. "Logical" here does not mean what Bloom et al. mean by "logical." Standards of "clear thinking" or "formal logic" are not the standards which are being referred to. The appropriate standards and criteria for judging performances which indicate a particular mental ability are those which characterize the various forms of knowledge, such as history, science, mathematics and so on. As we argued in the preceding section, each of these forms have criteria peculiar to them by which we can assess our judgments as to what is the case, i.e., according to which we may or may not legitimately make a claim to know something in history or science or mathematics. Thus, the criteria for deciding whether or not Marx was a "cause" of the 1917 Revolution are very different from the criteria for judging that the moon "causes" the tidal ebb and flow. The criteria for deciding whether it is wrong to tell a lie are distinct from those according to which one may legitimately judge or claim to know that a psychopath's behavior is a result of his repressed attitude toward his father. There is nothing wrong with saying that someone has an ability to make these judgments, or that he is exercising such mental skills as "comprehension," "analysis," "synthesis" and so on in doing so. The trouble is that we are saying so little unless we refer to the particular logical criteria which differentiate one kind of analysis, one kind of synthesis, from another. And there is the further danger that, when we speak merely of mental abilities and skills without logically differentiating them, we imply that skills at analysis or synthesis in one form of knowledge is transferred to another. But while it may help us to be skilled in literary critical analysis when we come to do philosophical or historical analysis, there is certainly not enough carry-over to permit us to speak of an undifferentiated "analytical ability."

(D) "KNOWING HOW" AND "KNOWING THAT"

Gilbert Ryle's distinction between "knowing how" and "knowing that" is a distinction rather like Bloom's between "knowing how to make judgments about what is or is not true" and "knowing information." Ryle's main statement of the practical implications of his distinction seem unexceptionable enough.

> In ordinary life . . . as well as in the special business of teaching, we are much more concerned with people's competences than with their cognitive repertoires, with the operations rather than with the truths that they learn. Indeed, even when we are concerned with their intellectual excellences and deficiencies, we are interested less in the stocks of truths that they acquire and retain than in their capacities to find out truths for themselves and their ability to organize them and exploit them, when discovered. Often we deplore a person's ignorance of some fact only because we deplore the stupidity of which his ignorance is a part.[18]

Although there is little to protest in this statement, we think it is important to reject the suggestion that "knowing information" and "knowing stocks of truths" is separable from the ability to make judgments about what makes a particular fact a "fact" or a particular truth "true." As an extension of our previous argument in the previous section we will now maintain that no one can be said to "know" a fact or "know" a truth unless he is able to back up his judgment that the particular "fact" or "truth" *is* true.

[18] Gilbert Ryle, *The Concept of Mind* (Middlesex, England: Penguin Books Ltd., 1949), pp. 28–29.

But first we ought to consider Ryle's aversion to such terms as "judgment" which refer to "mental acts." The reasons for Ryle's aversion to such terms may be found in his denial that "a man who believes that the earth is round must from time to time be going through some unique procedure of cognizing, judging or internally reasserting with a feeling of confidence 'the earth is round.'"[19] As Ryle quite rightly points out, we can only tell whether a man knows or believes something if certain of his performances come up to certain standards. Nevertheless, Ryle would surely agree that in order to test a man's claim to "know that x is the case" we might want him to do more than merely *say* "x is the case." Thus, for example, we might want to test him to see if he could provide evidence to support his claim that "x is the case," and we might also want to test him to make sure that he has the concept of "x." We gave an example of such tests before when we wanted to find out if a man knew that London is the capital of England. And we want to insist that there is nothing inappropriate about saying that the man is backing up his *judgment* that "London is the capital of England."

We need to insist on this when we read in Ryle's *The Concept of Mind* that

> . . . the styles and procedures of people's activities *are* the way their minds work and are not merely imperfect reflections of the postulated secret processes which were supposed to be the workings of minds.[20]

This is an overstatement which amounts to a mistake. We may only be able to *tell* what someone "thinks" or what is "in his mind" from the styles and procedures of his activities (including speaking and writing). But the test for a mental performance is not the same as the mental performance itself. The only way we can find out that a man has made a judgment, had an idea or discovered a solution is through his public perfor-

19 Ibid., p. 44.
20 Ibid., p. 58.

mances. This does not mean that we should equate what he does publicly with his mental activities.

Ryle rarely goes so far as to suggest that he holds this extreme view, and it would not be necessary to take Ryle to task if this element in his thinking had not misled educationists. Unfortunately it has formed the basis of an article in Smith and Ennis' important and influential collection *Language and Concepts in Education,* an article which lends support to some crucial misconceptions about knowledge in education. Jane Roland[21] interprets Ryle as maintaining or implying that "knowing that" sentences are "translatable into" or "reducible to" "knowing how" sentences. She argues that to say that someone "knows that *x* is the case" means only that certain of his performances come up to certain standards or that they would if he were tested. The shorthand phrase is to say that "knowing that" is "dispositional"—for someone to "know that" means only that he has a "disposition" or "tendency" to perform in certain ways. The corollary of this is to deny that it makes sense to talk about a "mental act" of judgment being associated with "knowing that." While Ryle never actually says at any point that "knowing that" is analyzable dispositionally, we have noted that he leans very markedly in this direction. It is essential that we support our view that it is meaningful to speak of "knowing that" being associated with mental acts of judgment if we are to avoid Roland's crucial mistakes about the nature of knowledge in education; mistakes which we will try to expose.

Ryle's account of dispositions has been subjected to effective criticism by Geach in his provocatively titled book, *Mental Acts.*[22] His demolition of Ryle's "reckless" use of the term "disposition" will be our starting point for exposing Roland's misconceptions about the nature of knowledge in education. Geach examines Ryle's key example of the brittleness of glass,

[21] Jane Roland, "On the Reduction of 'Knowing That' to 'Knowing How,'" in *Language and Concepts in Education,* eds. B. O. Smith and R. H. Ennis (Skokie, Illinois: Rand McNally and Co., 1962).

[22] Peter Geach, *Mental Acts* (London: Routledge and Kegan Paul, Ltd., 1957).

as what he means by a "disposition." Ryle argues that to say that glass is brittle is to say that if it ever is or had been struck or strained, it would fly or have flown into fragments.[23] In his analogy with someone knowing or believing that the earth is round, Ryle maintains that there is no reference to internal states of cognizing, judging or internally reasserting with a feeling of confidence, "the earth is round." The belief is evidenced in what a man says or does. It is not an internal mental event any more than the brittleness of glass is internal to the glass.

Geach makes two main points. First, he denies that the brittleness of glass is adequately analyzed by saying that if one does certain things to it a certain hypothetical becomes true of it, i.e., it breaks. He points out that the success of the principle upon which scientists work—that there is a need to look for *actual* differences between, for example, a magnetized and an unmagnetized bit of iron—is obviously more than mere luck. It is certainly not enough to characterize the difference by saying that if certain things are done to a bit of iron, certain hypotheticals become true of it.

Second, Geach points out that we would be extremely reluctant to regard a statement that two men whose overt behavior was not actually different were in different states of mind as really being a statement that the behavior of one of them *would have been* different from the other in hypothetical circumstances. Examples of this are endless but since Geach's point is highly concentrated, one might help. If we read two children two different stories, one about ghastly doings in a charnelhouse, the other about the triumph of Sir Lancelot over his enemies, their overt behavior in both cases may be rapt attention. If we were to say that they were in different states of mind we would not be saying that one's behavior would have been different from the other under certain hypothetical circumstances, whatever these may be. Geach maintains that it is not merely permissible but often essential to talk about "mental acts" such as "cognizing," "judging" and so on. The only evi-

[23] Ryle, *The Concept of Mind*, p. 43.

dence we have that such mental acts take place is in what people do and say. However their performances are not the same thing as their judgments.

Our objections to Roland's dispositional account of "knowing that" go further than this, however. Not merely does she want to reduce "knowing that" to "knowing how," her most serious error is to translate "knowing that" sentences into a very *limited* range of "knowing how" sentences—into "knowing how to answer a question or state a fact."[24] It is this restriction which leads her into errors very similar to those which we have described in Bloom's *Taxonomy*. To refer again to the example we used then: if a man claimed to know that "London is the capital of England" we might expect him not only to say this, but also to provide us with evidence that what he is offering is a judgment rather than merely repeating something by rote and we might expect him to pass tests to show that he has the concept of "a capital."

The disastrous consequences of Roland's restriction of the tests for "knowing that" to "knowing how to answer a question or state a fact" are apparent if we look at the conclusion to her article. There we find her acceptance of a quite untenable distinction between a subject (such as history) as a body of knowledge or collection of facts and history as an activity. As if someone who had learned to parrot off lists of dates, events and so on could be said to *know* that everything he parroted off *was* the case, before any testing of whether he understood what he was talking about or whether he could provide any evidence for his claims.

There can be no valid distinction of the sort which Roland is making (and which constantly recurs in popular writing about education) between teaching, say, history as a "body of knowledge" and teaching history as an "activity." If it is *history* that is being taught, i.e., that form of knowledge called history, then both the procedures of inquiry and the body of knowledge must be being passed on. We cannot claim to have taught someone history if he is incapable of substantiating what he

[24] Roland, "On the Reduction of . . .," *Language and Concepts in Education.*, p. 62.

says he knows about the past or does not understand what he is talking about when he uses terms such as "Industrial Revolution," "Renaissance" and so on. Of course it is unusual for someone to be completely ignorant of what he says he knows about the past. Merely making correct statements about the past or about anything else is by no means a guarantee that someone knows them to be true. To the extent to which someone fails to pass the "evidence" test and the "concept" test we deny that he knows.

(E) WHAT ARE THE "FACTS"?

Jane Roland's difficulties may stem largely from her very sloppy use of the term "fact" and in this, too, her writing is representative of a great deal of writing about education. There was a time when "facts" were alleged to be a very important part of the content of education (cf. the Hadow Report of 1931—"Knowledge to be acquired and facts to be stored") though they have suffered a decline in popularity since the advent of "activity." These fashions depend to some extent on a loose grasp of the very slippery concept of a "fact."

Since Roland's use of "fact" is representative of current writing on education, it will be instructive to examine what she says with some care. For Roland there seems to be one governing condition for something to be a "fact"—that it be "obvious" or "beyond question." The sort of "fact" she has in mind is that for which a minimum of evidence is necessary and the knowledge of which involves little judgment. The best case of this restriction of the concept is one she borrows from Ryle, who was also rather confused about "facts." The example is, "knowing that *messer* is the German word for 'knife.'" Let us see what is involved in knowing this "fact."

There is a sense in which we might say, for example, that a parrot could know the German word for "knife"—a sense which is analogous to saying that a parrot knows "Waltzing Matilda." A human being who can sing "Waltzing Matilda" despite the fact that he does not understand English (or Australian) would be in roughly the position of a parrot who could

sing it. All that is meant is that the parrot can recall the words
and the tune. In this sense one might be said to know the
German word for "knife" if he can say *messer* even without
knowing what it means. All that this implies is that he knows a
word and can pronounce it. This is the sense in which the
parrot knows a word—the parrot can pronounce it. But a
parrot could not be said to know that the German word for
"knife" is *messer*, for this involves a judgment of which a parrot
is incapable. A parrot cannot know what a "knife" is, what
"German" is or what "English" is—it could have none of these
concepts. A German child learning to speak his native language
may find the judgment "this is a *messer* and not a dagger" a
difficult one. A further step is involved in understanding or
judging that this word "knife" is English and that it means
messer. It is absurd to say that there are no skills or operations
involved in knowing that the German word for "knife" is
messer, yet Roland contrasts this "factual proposition" with, for
example, "knowing how to play chess" and "knowing how to
speak Russian" on the grounds that the latter, but not the
former, involves "skills and operations."

We do not deny that there is an important difference
between, for example, knowing German words and knowing
how to speak German. The difference between such competences has been referred to by Professor Passmore as a difference between "closed" and "open" competences.[25] "Speaking
German" involves moving beyond skills that one has been
directly and explicitly taught. When a person begins to say German sentences which he has made up for himself he is beginning to exercise an "open" competence—these involve originality of some sort. But it must be insisted that knowing how to
translate single words from one language to another *is* a competence and does involve a judgment. It is merely a necessary
test of someone's knowledge that he can recall and repeat the
word (for the parrot can do this too). A sufficient test that he
knows it is the right translation of an English word would be
much more complex (cf. our test for whether a man knows that
London is the capital of England).

[25] For a fuller account of this distinction see pp. 155–56 below.

Roland employs several examples to suggest that knowing facts is not a skill or a competence and does not involve a judgment. The point is sufficiently important to warrant methodical analysis of each one. The example she uses on page 61 of her article—knowing that Sussex is a county in England—is also borrowed from Ryle and is open to objections similar to those raised against the previous example. But the example on the following page, "Johnny knows that Columbus discovered America," is different. The knowledge required in this case is not knowledge of an arbitrary linguistic convention but knowledge of the occurrence of an actual event. It is this sort of thing that people generally have in mind when they speak of facts. It is sensible to ask for evidence to support a claim to knowledge of this kind. (Whereas it is odd to ask for the evidence that *messer* means "knife." All we can reply is "That's what Germans *say* when they refer to what we call a knife.") If Johnny does *know* that Columbus discovered America, he must be able to reply to the question, "How do you know?" with something better than "teacher told me that Columbus discovered it." As it happens it is doubtful whether or not Columbus *did* discover America, and evidence to the effect that he did is indispensable for claiming to know that this event took place. We are not suggesting that in order to claim to know, for example, that in England the Second World War began in 1939 we have to consult the newspapers of that year and look up the official records. The evidence for this fact is so readily available that we may safely assume that it is true. If anyone were to ask Britons how they know that World War II began in 1939 they would quite legitimately ask him why on earth he should doubt it, pointing out, perhaps, that the evidence is there if you ask people who are over thirty-five years old. This is quite different from someone asking us how we know that the Second Peloponnesian War was in 369 B.C. We would feel obliged to refer to our sources, to the archaeological evidence and so on.

In none of these cases would it be correct to say, as Roland does, that it is translatable into the form, "Johnny knows how to answer the question correctly." Even in the case of "knowing that the Second World War began in 1939" there are many children who do not know what "1939" means, have only the vaguest notions about the Second World War and yet who could certainly answer correctly the question, "When did it begin?"

Roland's final examples of "knowing factual propositions" are once again logically distinct from the previous varieties of "facts."[26] They are observation statements—witnessing a murder and "knowing who the murderer is" and looking at the rain falling and "knowing that the rain is falling." We must acknowledge that in such cases it seems to be an overstatement to refer to the knowledge as being related to a "judgment." One can *see* who the murderer is, see the rain falling. We are quite rightly reluctant to dignify such directly acquired knowledge by referring to them as "judgments."

If such examples, however, strike us as being "judgments" only in an extended sense of "judgment," and are thus awkward cases for our analysis, they are even more awkward for Roland to handle. Consider what happens when we try her "translation" from "knowing that" to "knowing how" on the pattern she employed with the "Columbus discovered America" example. On that pattern, "Jones knows that it is raining" is equivalent to saying that "Jones can correctly answer the question, 'Is it raining?'" Are we to conclude then that a dog does not know that it is raining when it sees and feels the rain? Of course the dog cannot call it "rain," but what if we taught a parrot to correctly answer the question, "Is it raining?" that is, whenever the parrot saw the rain outside it said, in reply to our question, "It is raining." Surely we would not maintain that, in such a case, answering the question correctly is equivalent to knowing that it is raining. If parrots (or dogs) can be said to "know" that it is raining, they can be said to "know" it independently of any "remarks" that they might make.

We have examined every example of "facts" which Roland mentions to show that despite the considerable variety of examples, each one involves the minimum element of judgment and a concomitantly negligible need for evidence. "Knowing

[26] Roland, "On the Reduction of . . . ," *Language and Concepts in Education* p. 62.

facts" is thus caricatured by Roland as knowing the simplest and most obvious sorts of facts. It is only thus that she is able to maintain in her conclusion that there is a significant contrast between (a) teaching history as a body of knowledge or collection of facts independent of evidence and (b) teaching history as an activity or skill with a concern for substantiating claims to knowledge by reference to evidence. The contrast between the two approaches is not important because it is basically factitious. Teaching historical facts, as Roland represents them, is a side issue in history teaching. We have pointed out that even the teaching of dates in history is a far more complex matter than getting children to recite them. Of course, a child cannot be said to "know that the Russian Revolution began in 1917" unless he can *say* that it did. But his simply reciting it is no guarantee that he knows it. There are many fourteen-year-old children who simply do not know even what "1969" means. They know that every year this number grows by one, but "fifty years ago" is a mysterious notion for many children. It is for this reason that history teachers use devices such as "time lines" to give children the concept of a date like "1917."

We will conclude this discussion by pointing to one or two difficulties with "facts" which have been the subject of philosophic debate and which might make us even more careful about employing this concept. We have maintained that Roland's association of "facts" with a body of knowledge such as history rubs shoulders uneasily with the other way she mentions "facts" such as, "It is raining." Part of the problem is the various ways in which "facts" may relate to "reality." J. L. Austin, in his article "Unfair to Facts" maintains that

> When 'facts' or 'a fact' occur in general in modern English, the usage is just what it was in the eighteenth century. When we say, 'the mangy condition of the cat is a fact' we mean it is an actual state of affairs; when we say, 'What are the facts?' we mean 'What is the actual state of affairs?,' what has actually occurred? or the like.[27]

[27] *J. L. Austin, Philosophical Papers,* ed. J. O. Urmson and G. J. Warnock (Oxford: Oxford University Press, 1961) p. 113.

Austin contrasts this usage with that of a philosopher such as Strawson who maintains that, "Facts are what statements (when true) state; they are not what statements are about."[28]

Austin and Strawson debate the propriety of saying that "facts" are "in the world" or "actual" rather than equivalent to the more general notion of "what is true." Is the "fact" that it is raining the water out there falling on the lawn or is the "fact" the *statement* "It is raining," when this is correct? Roland never sees this difficulty, and she may well have profited from paying more attention to the ordinary sense of "knowing facts" as knowing something that actually occurred. What gives strength to the fact that it is raining is that it can be *seen* to be raining. The evidence is an inseparable *part* of knowing that it is raining if you are seeing it fall. Knowing this fact is not merely equivalent to correctly stating it. The lesson to be learned about the more "remote" facts of history, geography, science and so on is the necessity for us to grasp them as *actualities* for us to say that we *know* the facts. The evidence for such "remote" facts is not as tightly bound up with them as is the evidence for "It's raining." But the evidence brings out the actuality of facts and gives us the warrant for saying that we know them.

We have made the following points in this section:

(1) There is no valid distinction between "knowing facts" and "knowing how to make judgments about what is the case." A student's knowledge of facts (as distinct from his ability to recite factual propositions) logically depends on his understanding what he means when he asserts something to be the case and upon his ability to produce sufficient evidence to warrant his claim to know that something is the case. It is equally mistaken to refer to teaching history or science as an "activity" or as "the imparting of facts and information," for getting children to know facts necessarily involves them in various mental activities.

(2) It is plain from (1) that there are no grounds for maintaining that *all* that is meant by "knowing" something is

[28] See Ibid., p. 116.

that one is capable of satisfying certain tests. We are testing various sorts of mental performances, in particular, "judging." Teachers are fundamentally concerned with getting children to make correct judgments about what is the case in various forms of knowledge. This endeavor necessarily involves the teachers in getting children to make judgments and to know *how* to make judgments.

SECTION(A)

Basic References

HIRST, P. H., "Liberal Education and the Nature of Knowledge," *Philosophical Analysis and Education*, ed. R. D. Archambault, London: Routledge and Kegan Paul, Ltd., 1965.

PETERS, R. S., *Ethics and Education*, Chapter 5 and Part I, Section 5. London: Allen and Unwin, Ltd., 1966.

Further References

NEWMAN, J. H., *On the Scope and Nature of University Education*. London: J. M. Dent & Sons, Ltd., 1915.

OAKESHOTT, M., "The Voice of Poetry in the Conversation of Mankind," *Rationalism and Politics and Other Essays*, London: Methuen, 1962.

PHOENIX, P. H., *Realms of Meaning*, Part 2. New York: McGraw-Hill Book Company, 1964.

Essay/Discussion Topics

* I am asked what is the end of University Education . . . I answer that . . . knowledge is capable of being its own end . . . any kind of knowledge, if it really be such, is its own reward. . . . Knowledge is not merely a means to something beyond it, or the preliminary of certain arts into which it naturally resolves, but an end sufficient . . . to pursue for its own sake. (Newman, J. H., *On the Scope and Nature of University Education*, pp. 93–4.)

Discuss.

* How does R. S. Peters' account of the content of education in terms of its "cognitive perspective" differ from P. H. Hirst's account of the content of education? Can the two views be reconciled?

SECTION (B)

References

The literature on the "logic" of various forms of knowledge is large and various. See the Appendix for some suggested reading under subject headings.

Essay/Discussion Topics

* Compare the logical characteristics of any two disciplines in which you have received some training with reference to any of the following characteristics.

(1) The nature of the key concepts which are distinctive of each subject.
(2) The characteristic relations between the key concepts in each subject.
(3) The criteria according to which judgments are assessed for truth or falsity within each subject.

SECTION (C)

Basic References

BLOOM, B. S. et al., *Taxonomy of Educational Objectives,* Vol. I, Chapter 2, and *Condensed Taxonomy,* pp. 201–207. London: Longmans, Green & Co., Ltd., 1956.

HIRST, P. H., "Liberal Education and the Nature of Knowledge," *Philosophical Analysis and Education.*

Further References

General Education in a Free Society: Report of the Harvard Committee. London: Oxford University Press, 1946.

Arts and Science Sides in the Sixth Form: Gulbenkian Foundation Report. London: Oxford University Department of Education, 1960.

RYLE, G., *The Concept of Mind,* particularly pp. 124–26. Middlesex, England: G. B. Penguin Books, Ltd., 1963.

Essay/Discussion Topics

* The training is to be one in the sensitive and scrupulous use of intelligence. . . . Valid analytic practice is a strengthening of the sense of relevance; . . . all appropriate play of intelligence, being also an exercise of the sense of value, is controlled by an implicit concern for a total value-judgment. (F. R. Leavis, *Education and the University,* [London: Chatto and Windus, Ltd., 1961,] p. 71.)

This is an account by a leading practitioner of literary criticism of the "abilities" which are trained by this discipline. Evaluate this or any other similar account of the "abilities" which are alleged to be developed by a subject with which you are familiar.

* Read pages 124–26 of *The Concept of Mind,* by Gilbert Ryle. If we accept a more general view of "ability" as being equivalent to "can" or "is able," what qualifications would need to be made of the analysis which was presented in section (C) of the preceding chapter?

SECTIONS (D) AND (E)

Basic References

ROLAND, J., "On the Reduction of 'Knowing That' to 'Knowing How,'" *Language and Concepts in Education,* eds. B. O. Smith and R. H. Ennis. Skokie, Illinois: Rand McNally and Co., 1962.

RYLE, G., "Knowing How and Knowing That" *Philosophy and Education,* ed. I. Scheffler, 2nd ed. Boston: Allyn and Bacon, Inc., 1966.

Further References

AUSTIN, J. L., "Unfair to Facts," *Philosophical Papers,* eds. J. O. Urmson and G. J. Warnock. Oxford: Oxford University Press, 1961.

GRIFFITHS, A. P. ed., *Knowledge and Belief*. Oxford: Oxford University Press, 1967.

HERBST, P., "The Nature of Facts," *Essays in Conceptual Analysis,* ed. A. Flew. London: Macmillan and Co., Ltd., 1956.

HIRST, P. H., "Logical and Psychological Aspects of Teaching a Subject," *The Concept of Education,* ed. R. S. Peters. London: Routledge and Kegan Paul, Ltd., 1967.

RYLE, G., *The Concept of Mind.*

SCHEFFLER, I., *Conditions of Knowledge,* Chapters 1 and 5. Chicago: Scott, Foresman and Co., 1965.

Essay/Discussion Topics

* Is Ryle's distinction between "knowing how" and "knowing that" a useful one in educational discussion?

> * Whitehead said that a merely well-informed man is the most useless bore on God's earth. I do not entirely agree. I always find encyclopaedias interesting. Equally boring, in my view, are those for whom being critical is a substitute for being well informed about anything. To parody Kant: content without criticism is blind, but criticism without content is empty. (R. S. Peters, "Education as Initiation.") [*Philosophical Analysis and Education,* ed. R. D. Archambault, London, Routledge and Kegan Paul Ltd., 1965, p. 104.]

We have tended to ignore the "merely well-informed man," the "Quiz King." Can he *know* his content without criticism?

4

Further
Psychological
Considerations
in Education

LET US CONSIDER some alternative views of
the teacher's basic concerns as seen through the eyes of educational psychologists. Since most of the readers of this book will
be studying educational psychology as well as educational
philosophy we ought to consider the very different approaches
of educational psychology textbooks to such matters as the
nature of the teacher's role. Of course there are limits to the
extent that we can pursue the psychologists. Time and time
again we are pulled up short when we read educational psychology by remarks "en passant" such as Professor Morris'
"flight into impersonal study is one form of defense, and
equally, flight from a disciplined rationality is another."[1] There
are so many assumptions packed into this statement that the
job of unpacking would almost be as formidable as tackling the
deepseated prejudices and bland superiority of a man such as
George W. Hartmann, a quotation from whose *Educational*

[1] J. W. Tibble (ed.), *The Study of Education* (London: Routledge and
Kegan Paul; New York: The Humanities Press, 1966) p. 171.

Psychology appears as the first question for discussion at the end of this chapter.

We propose to concentrate on a few concepts in educational psychology, partly because they are important ones, partly because they are ones which can be usefully analyzed without the necessity of coming to grips with the grass roots assumptions of the various schools of psychological thought. In the first section we will consider the widespread use in educational psychology of such related concepts as "needs," "self-realization" and "mental health." In the later section we will try a philosophical invasion of the psychological preserves of "intelligence" and "creativity."

(A) "MENTAL HEALTH" AND "SELF-REALIZATION" AS EDUCATIONAL AIMS

R. S. Peters offers a detailed analysis of " 'Mental Health' as an Educational Aim." Only one of his arguments is necessary in order to refute the view that mental health is an educational aim. He argues that a mentally healthy person may be completely uneducated. Peters imagines such a man as one who has plenty of food, sex, drink and security— "a pastoral life surrounded by the joys of the countryside."

> But when we spoke to him of the delicacies of human relationships, of art, or of the excitement of discovery, he might spit and say that we needed our brains tested. From a psychological point of view he might be mentally healthy, integrated, adjusted—all of these things—but at the level of what Plato called "the necessary appetites."[2]

To see the achievement of "mental health" as an educational aim is to sell éducation short. It is not a positive "end" of education, it is rather, as Peters suggests, a "negative council." Teachers ought to be on the lookout for children who suffer from such impediments to the achievement of "mental health" as the lack of food, love or security. Many psychologists see mental illness, neurosis and various forms of ineducability as

[2] " 'Mental Health' as an Educational Aim," *Aims in Education*, pp. 82–3.

resulting from such basic deprivations. Teachers can hardly avoid noticing this lack of mental health in its grosser forms. In his first years of teaching this writer was plagued by a boy who responded to no form of encouragement, no attempt to interest him. He seemed quite ineducable. But then his parents came to the school and his mother said to the teacher, in front of the child, "We didn't want him in the first place and we still don't want him." It is expecting far too much of teachers to think that they could or ought to do much about a child such as this. This is from no lack of sympathy. Who could not feel sorry for a child so deprived? Of course we usually do try to do something—we might even succeed in gaining the child's trust and affection—only to desert him at the end of the year when he moves to another class. Our inadequate and fumbling attempts to help children such as this must be replaced by the work of trained counselors or advisors. Certainly it would be a mistake to accept as one of the "aims" of education a function which teachers usually perform because there are no trained counselors in schools. In fact, "mental health" is usually advanced as one of the "needs" which ought to be satisfied in schools rather than as an "aim" of education. There is a wide variety of talk about "needs" in education, and we will return to "mental health" when we consider it as a "need" in the next section.

"Self-realization" and "personal growth," on the other hand, are often put forward as "aims of education." They are often associated with "mental health," but as Peters points out, "self-realization" and "growth" go beyond the minimal requirements for mental health.

> . . . though people may be missing a lot that they might find satisfying if they don't devote themselves to art, music and good causes, it would be odd to describe them as mentally ill.[3]

Nevertheless, Peters recognizes that "self-realization" and "growth" are more plausible educational aims than "mental health." The trouble with these concepts is that they are so indeterminate. "Self-realization" and "growth"

[3] Ibid., p. 83.

. . . presuppose standards of value which determine both the sort of self which is *worth* realizing and the *direction* of growth. Human beings are not like flowers in having a pre-determined end which serves as a final cause of their development. "Growing" or "realizing oneself" implies doing things which are thought to be worthwhile rather than others. The standards by reference to which they are judged to be worthwhile are grasped by men and handed on from generation to generation.[4]

Peters is not saying that it is completely pointless to refer to "growth" or "self-realization" as educational aims—it just doesn't get us very far until we begin to specify those activities which will realize the self in worthwhile ways or define the appropriate direction of growth. We attempted such a specification in the previous chapter when we maintained that the various forms of knowledge were the means by which the experience of children could be structured and organized in worthwhile ways. And we suggest that this specification makes the vague talk of "self-realization" or "growth" redundant in so far as these terms are used in arguments designed to affect the content of education.

But as Peters points out, it is not surprising that the advocate of such aims is usually unspecific about the content of education. His real concern is with *how* rather than with *what* we teach. The main object of such educational policies is to recommend a certain *manner* of education. In particular, the advocate of "self-realization" or "growth" will want to reject "authoritarian" methods of teaching. Instead of teaching methods being devised with reference to the different sorts of subject matter to be passed on, instead of discipline being imposed from above, he will devise methods on the basis of various sorts of "psychological" considerations. For example, he will look to the desires, needs, interests, experiences and wants of children in order to work out appropriate methods. In short, the advocates of "self-realization" or "growth" are much

[4] R. S. Peters, "Education as Initiation," in *Philosophical Analysis and Education,* ed. R. D. Archambault (London: Routledge and Kegan Paul, Ltd., 1965) pp. 94–5.

more likely to favor "child-centered" methods of teaching than ones which involve instruction and "teacher-centered" methods.

We are far from dismissing references to "self-realization" or "growth" as educational aims. Instead, we are reinterpreting such references as reflecting a concern for one of the necessary conditions of calling an activity an educational activity. The proponents of these "aims" are insisting in a confused and misleading way that every effort should be made to ensure that those being educated come to care about what they are doing. In the initial stages of learning, in particular the production of motivation and interest in what is to be learned depends largely on appropriate teaching *methods*.

If we examine the work of one of the leading advocates of "growth" or "self-realization," John Dewey, we find that he is basically against the use of "traditional," "authoritarian" teaching methods. When Dewey objects to the ". . . imposition from above and from outside of adult standards, subject matter, and methods upon those who are only growing slowly towards maturity"[5] it sounds as if he were objecting to the subject matter of traditional education. But this is not really so. Dewey's objection is to the necessity to *impose* subject matter which is "beyond the reach of the experience the young learners possess." Dewey is not questioning the view that the experience of the child is to be structured and organized through the various forms of knowledge. The conclusion to *The Child and the Curriculum* makes it quite explicit that in Dewey's view the appropriate subject matter of education is ultimately "those organized bodies of truth that we call studies." The teacher's wealth of knowledge operates as a goal and a culmination of the child's activities in the classroom.

> It is the child's present powers which are to assert themselves; his present capacities which are to be exercised; his present attitudes which are to be realized. But save as the teacher knows, wisely and thoroughly, the race-expression which is embodied in that thing we call the Curriculum, the teacher knows neither what the present power,

[5] *Experience and Education* (New York: Macmillan, 1959) p. 4.

capacity, or attitude is, not yet how it is to be asserted, exercised, and realized.[6]

Dewey's thinking here is very close to Peters' summary of the importance in education of the "psychological" considerations we have been examining:

> There are levels of development in childhood and damage can be done if even the basic skills of reading, writing and arithmetic are passed on too early; there are ways, too, of teaching skills which may be damaging. And the importance of such skills can be emphasized with complete disregard for basic needs like those of love and security. Warped and stunted children may result from foolish methods of teaching. This is where talk of mental health, of integration, and of wholeness is relevant as a negative council of great importance. It is something that educators should never neglect while they educate people.[7]

The negative emphasis of Peters' remarks distinguishes them from Dewey's, of course. Dewey inclines strongly towards the view that "authoritarian" teaching methods are necessarily bad and strongly insists on the necessity for teachers to employ methods which start from the experience and interests of the child in order to engage him actively in the learning process. The fact remains, however, that for some children and some subjects the most effective way of inducing interest in what they are doing may be to instruct, to adopt "authoritarian" methods.[8] While it is good advice to tell us to consider the experience, interests and desires of our pupils when we are working out teaching procedures, we may quite legitimately decide to ignore all this on some occasions. Some of our best lessons may be ones when we present, for example, a poem which is quite foreign to the children's experience and interests

---

[6] *The Child and the Curriculum,* (Chicago: University of Chicago Press, 1962) p. 31.

[7] Peters, "Mental Health as an Educational Aim," *Aims in Education,* p. 84.

[8] Dewey was not opposed to the notion that the teacher needs to be *"an* authority." But he was opposed to "authoritarian" methods of teaching. For a much fuller discussion of this distinction, see pp. 152–56.

but which shakes them out of their stock expectations and develops new interests.

(B) SOCIAL OR PSYCHOLOGICAL "NEEDS" IN EDUCATION[9]

. . . before everything else the school should provide for the pre-adolescent and adolescent years a life which answers to their special needs.[10]

Most textbooks on educational psychology devote a section to the "needs" of children which ought to be met by schools. There is, however, considerable variation among various writers as to what is meant by "needs." We will begin by classifying some of the main conceptions.

(1) *Needs-satisfaction as motivation for learning*. Pressey, Robinson and Horrocks, in their textbook *Psychology in Education*, refer to five categories of "needs," "from the most to the least basic":

1. Physiological needs, such as hunger and thirst.
2. Safety needs, such as protection from harm and injury.
3. Needs for affection and belongingness.
4. Esteem needs, such as self-respect and social approval.
5. Self-actualization in the sense of developing one's potentialities to their limit.

Pressey, Robinson and Horrocks comment as follows:

The teacher who wishes to motivate her pupils to fulfil the needs just described must remember the prepotency of the more basic needs and ensure that they are satisfied before she can expect the children to function wholeheartedly at the higher level. For example, a child who has missed his lunch, and is disliked by his teacher and the other children, and has failed so often that he doubts himself, can hardly

[9] I am indebted at several points in this section to a paper entitled "Needs" read by R. F. Dearden to the Philosophy of Education Society of Great Britain in 1965, and to which I replied.

[10] *The Spens Report* (London: H.M.S.O., Secondary Education, 1939) p. 149.

be expected to be overly interested in expressing himself through classroom activities in artistic self-expression.[11]

(2) *Need for "Mental Health."* C. M. Fleming defines "needs" as "those psychological requirements which are common to all human beings by virtue of their humanity." And she continues:

> The most significant of these appear to be:
>   the receiving of appreciation or affection,
>   (experience of being loved)
>   the sharing in co-operative endeavours,
>   (opportunities of making a contribution or participating),
> and the conditions contributing to growth—the meeting of new experiences, the chance to attain some measure of understanding or insight, and the exposure to suitable tuition in informational or other educational experiences.[12]

When Fleming later describes "the teacher's task," the first point she makes is that teachers are "concerned to direct the perceptions of pupils" through satisfying their psychological needs. In this respect Fleming hints at the notion of needs-satisfaction as motivation for learning. But her central contention is that the satisfaction of the "needs" she lists is necessary if children are to become (healthy) human beings. The notion of "mental health" is implicit: a child may lack "experience of being loved" and still become *human*—though he would very likely be emotionally disturbed.

(3) *Need for Socialization.* H. H. Giles, et al., in *Exploring the Curriculum*, attributes the following six major groups of "needs" to American adolescents as the basis for working out a curriculum:

    (i)   for establishing personal relationships
    (ii) for establishing independence
    (iii) for understanding human behaviour
    (iv) for establishing self in society

---

[11] S. L. Pressey, F. V. Robinson, and J. E. Horrocks, *Psychology in Education* (New York: Harper & Row, 1959) p. 208.

[12] C. M. Fleming, *Teaching—A Psychological Analysis* (London: Methuen & Co., Ltd., 1958) p. 32.

(v) for normality

(vi) for understanding the universe.[13]

Before we consider any of these proposals in detail, a fundamental objection arises when we consider them all together. Only three of the many "needs" advocates in the psychology of education have been accounted for and already we have a composite list of "needs" which, if they were all to be satisfied by schools, would mean teachers would have to take complete charge of a child. And yet schools are usually thought to have a primarily educational function, and it is difficult to see how this function can remain a primary one if schools take responsibility for looking after a child as parents, doctors, group leaders and so on are accustomed to do. Nor is it clear that teachers who are mainly only qualified to teach a subject are qualified to take on these varied responsibilities.

The response to this criticism might be that only *some* "needs" ought to be satisfied by schools. And then the whole game is given away. For it then follows that saying that something is a "need" is not equivalent to saying that it ought to be satisfied in schools. The question then becomes "How do we decide what ought to be done in schools?" No advocate of "needs-satisfaction" as the function of schools can afford to allow that some needs rather than others ought to be satisfied. This would involve the necessity of some other criterion to select among the "needs" to find out which ought to be the concern of schools. It would follow that references to "needs" would be of considerably less significance in education. And since selection among "needs" seems inevitable, the conclusion that references to "needs" are not crucial for deciding what ought to be done in schools seems inescapable.

It is plain that the authors of (1) and (2) would turn to what they call "basic needs" if it became necessary to select those "needs" which ought to be satisfied before all others. But whereas (1) insists that physiological needs are basic, as well as psychological needs, (2) makes no reference to physiologi-

[13] B. O. Smith, J. O. Stanley and W. H. Shores, *Fundamentals of Curriculum Development* (World Book Co., 1957) pp. 344–45.

cal needs at all. Presumably (2) ignores physiological needs on the ground that it is not the concern of educators to provide food, water and oxygen for children. While there might be some point in advising teachers to look out for children who are deprived in any of these respects, this is not to say that they are needs which ought to be satisfied by schools. We have also argued that this is the appropriate way for educators to concern themselves with those basic psychological needs to which (2) refers. Although teachers are well advised to keep an eye open for the emotionally disturbed or deprived child with a view to finding appropriate treatment for him, it is not the concern of teachers to provide, for example, "experience of being loved." In general, children don't *need* the teacher's love. And in those sad cases where they do, it may be an indication that the child should receive expert and reliable psychological attention.

The satisfaction of children's basic psychological needs, though it is not properly the teacher's job, does have a kind of priority however. The satisfaction of basic psychological needs is, on the psychological evidence available, a necessary condition of "mental health" and of educability. As Peters puts it,

> . . . unless we satisfy our needs for love and safety we shall be forever at sixes and sevens with ourselves, not satisfying a variety of wants properly because of conflict and indecision, or suffering from strange fears and distorted wants which cloud our perceptions and warp our judgement.[14]

The teacher has a clear obligation to make sure that such fundamentally deprived children receive the appropriate attention, both for their own sake and so that he, the teacher, can get on with the educational job. But it is far from clear whether or not a teacher should play a positive part in satisfying children's social "needs," assuming for the moment that reference to these is intelligible.

It is clearer that a teacher *could* do something about engineering the social interactions of his children than that he

---

[14] " 'Mental Health' as an Educational Aim," *Aims in Education,* p. 80.

could towards providing for their basic psychological needs. But it is less obvious that he *ought* to concern himself with them. "Social approval," "cooperative endeavor" and so on are not needed in such a critical way—if they are needed at all. Underlying such talk of "social needs" is an ideal which Jacques Barzun once referred to disparagingly as "the ideal of the harmonious committee." Such a preference for "cooperation" and "belongingness" should not masquerade as a "need." Perhaps we should watch out for the child who persistently fails or who seems very lonely to see if more suitable arrangements can be made for him. But such negative advice to a teacher is a long way from describing a "need" which teachers ought to take positive steps to satisfy—by means of group manipulation, project work and so on—on behalf of all the children he teaches.

This reference to the *methods* which might be advocated as a means of encouraging an arbitrarily chosen form of social adaptation brings out the important point that "needs" policies are directed more towards advocating certain *methods* of teaching than towards the advocation of a particular content for education. In the previous section, we noted that "mental health" and "self-realization" are usually advanced as "aims of education" in order to advocate "child-centered" methods of teaching. Similarly, when we find "self-actualization" in the sense of developing one's potentialities to their limit advanced as a "need" we are left completely in the dark about content. Do we not have potentialities for what is bad? Surely we do not *need* to develop these potentialities? "The conditions contributory to growth" is similarly vague—for growth in what direction? "Understanding and insight" and "informational experiences" are also useless as directives for the content of education. Such generalizations could be applicable to the content of the teaching in Fagin's school for young pickpockets. The vagueness of so-called "needs" for "normality" and "understanding the universe" needs no stressing.

References to "needs," then, fail to help us in characterizing the content of education. The psychologist offers no alternative analysis of the nature of the worthwhile activities which are to compose education to the one which we advanced in the previous chapter. But perhaps by referring to "needs" we may find principles which are relevant to the methodological problem of *motivating* children to engage in what is worthwhile. In a rather confused way, this is what is suggested by Pressey, Robinson and Horrocks. They seem to be putting forward two proposals:

(i) that teachers ought to motivate children to *fulfil* their "needs." This is surely very odd. We do not need to *motivate* children to satisfy their hunger or thirst or to seek affection.

(ii) that teachers should fulfil children's "needs" *as a means* of *motivating* them to engage in classroom activities.

The latter suggestion is based on a misconception. The well-fed, well-loved, self-respecting, widely admired, unharmed child may show little interest in "classroom activities," while the underfed, unhappy isolate may turn to history or science or "artistic self-expression" with great eagerness once he grasps their intrinsic interest. This in no way denies the point that severe deprivation of food or affection will usually lead to ineducability. Such ineducability, however, need not be a matter of lack of motivation—it relates to more fundamental factors relating to "mental health" and rationality. The only way in which the satisfaction of children's basic physiological or psychological "needs" could be used as motivation for learning would be to make their satisfaction conditional upon the learning. (E.g., keep the children from the taps and lavatories until they get their sums right!) If teachers were in a position to motivate children in this way, it would be immoral for them to do so.

The main points which have been advanced in this section are as follows:

(i) Confronted with the great variety of "needs" put forward by various writers it is necessary to ask which needs ought to be satisfied in schools. We are then asking for alternative principles for determining what ought to be done in schools.

(ii) The satisfaction of basic physiological and psychological needs is a necessary precondition of educability. Teachers ought to be aware that some children may suffer severe deprivation in these respects in order that the teachers may refer the children to those qualified to provide the necessary treatment.

(iii) References to "social needs" of various kinds conceal more or less undefended value judgments about what sort of social relationships are desirable. There is no warrant for speaking of "needs" in these matters unless these judgments are defended.

(iv) "Needs" policies reflect a concern with the method rather than with the content of education. But they are of very limited use even with regard to such methodological problems as motivation.

(C) INTELLIGENCE AND EDUCATION

Thus far we have been defending our view of what makes education worthwhile against several apparently conflicting views put forward both explicitly and implicitly by educational psychologists. In what follows, we will advance from this defensive position to invade some psychological citadels. The nature of "intelligence" has received more attention from educational psychologists than perhaps any other matter, and it is time that philosophers of education began to ask some leading questions. One of the major deterrents for philosophers in this area is the complexity of the psychological literature on the subject, as even a glance at the excellent selection in the Penguin book *Intelligence and Ability* (ed. Stephen Wiseman, 1967) will show. We will be referring to a discussion between two leading philosophers, P. H. Nowell-Smith and A. Mac-Intyre (in *The Aristotelian Society Proceedings,* Supplementary Volume, XXIV, 1960), and it is apparent from what they say about intelligence tests that they have in mind the Stanford-Binet test. This test is not widely used now, and some of their remarks about intelligence tests are not applicable to more recent tests. We are aware that philosophical discussion of a topic which involves a good deal of acquaintance with recent work in psychology runs the risk of being superficial. But the risk is worth running if we can succeed in provoking psychologists into clarifying what they *do* mean when they employ a concept such as "intelligence."

Our concern is to look for the rules which govern the use of "intelligent" and "intelligence." To some extent we will be interested in finding out what the rules are for using these terms in everyday discourse. Seeing this, the psychologist may stalk off contemptuously saying that he is concerned with *measuring* something, and the connections between what he means by intelligence and what the man in the street means by intelligence are about as uninteresting as the connections between mass and force in scientific and everyday discourse. While we can see what he means, we insist that there is an important difference. Given the vast amount of moral, political and ideological axe grinding associated with the notion of intelligence we should surely be reluctant to allow a special scientific use of the term "intelligence" to be employed without getting clear just *how* it relates to the concept of "intelligence" in ordinary usage. Unlike such terms as "mass" and "force," we want to know *what* everyday concept the scientific notion of intelligence is making precise.

What is intelligence? This is the sort of question which is likely to make psychologists shudder, and not without some justification. As Robinson remarks in his book *Definition*, the question formula, "What is *x*?" is the vaguest of all question forms except an inarticulate grunt. He adds that it is a question form which flourishes precisely because it is vague—it saves us the trouble of thinking out and saying exactly what we want to know about "*x*." Furthermore, one of the dangers in talking about "intelligence," the noun, is that we may be misled into thinking that it is a "thing," and it is far from clear that there is a "thing" called "intelligence."[15]

Let us ask, instead, for criteria for employing the adjective "intelligent." The sort of question which will preoccupy us will be, "What are samples of intelligent behavior?" "Can we say

<hr>

[15] See *Intelligence and Ability*, ed. Stephen Wiseman (Middlesex, England: G. B. Penguin Books, Ltd., 1967) pp. 159–76.

that a machine is intelligent?" "Can routine behavior be said to be intelligent or unintelligent?"

(i) *"Intelligent" is a disposition word* like "proud," "cheerful" or "cunning." We have already considered what Ryle means by referring to some words as "disposition" words (see pp. 61–62). In order to attribute any of these qualities to someone, it is not necessary that he be at any particular moment proud or cheerful or cunning or intelligent, but only that he is *disposed* to act in ways which make these descriptions appropriate. When we say that Johnny in 4B is "intelligent," we mean that if he is placed in particular circumstances he will produce responses of a particular kind. For example, if he is examined in "speed and accuracy" arithmetic tests, he will supply answers rapidly and accurately. If he offends a bad-tempered teacher he will find ways of soothing him and avoiding the painful consequences. If presented with a Chinese puzzle or a difficult riddle he will find the solution rapidly.

It is obviously helpful to think of "intelligent" as a "disposition" word because it concentrates our attention on the *behavior* which people must exhibit in order to be called intelligent. But we have already shown that Ryle's account of "dispositions" is not entirely satisfactory. It could lead us to ignore the *actual* differences between people by referring only to potential differences. Phrases which we often use such as "Johnny has a quick mind" or "Johnny thinks very fast" would always be translatable into statements such as "Under conditions x, Johnny will perform action y quickly and accurately." If we were to accept this, we might be led to ignore the evidence of neurologists and geneticists who maintain that these potentialities are related to actual differences in brain structure or genetic inheritance. While such evidence is of very little interest to our main concern—to get clear what sorts of behavior count as "intelligent"—it can be an important consideration in determining educational provisions. If, indeed, the capacity to be "intelligent" is an inborn or inherited disposition, we may be less eager to press ahead with naive expectations about the way an educational environment will improve children's capacity to act and think intelligently.

(ii) *Can machines be intelligent?* The author can remember having once maltreated an adding machine which seemed
incapable of cross-checking school attendances for the year
and may even have referred to it as a "stupid damn machine."
But if anyone had asked him if he *really* thought it to be stupid
he'd have assumed this was a bad joke. Nevertheless we might
sometimes say of what a chess playing machine does, "That's a
good move" or even "That's an intelligent move" or "That's a
stupid move." (Presumably we could only say the latter when
the machine does in a cog or has an electronic seizure.) But we
would surely never say that the machine *is* intelligent. If
someone were to remark, after we'd said of the machine's move
that it was an intelligent move, "Yes, well this is a very intelligent machine, you know," we would say something like, "Now
hold on, I didn't mean that the machine was intelligent, only
that it made a good move, the sort of move which if made by a
human being would be intelligent, but when made automatically is only a 'good' or 'bad' move." No amount of intricacy
in the machine would lead us to say of it that it was intelligent.

A similar ambiguity may arise with regard to human
beings. On an icy road the good driver turns into a skid to stop
the tail of his car from swinging around. The beginning driver
sitting next to him, realizing what the maneuver has accomplished, says, "Now that was an intelligent thing to do!" The
experienced driver may ask what on earth he's talking about,
and it may be necessary to describe his entirely "automatic"
behavior to him before he even realizes that he has done anything exceptional. We would not be saying anything odd if we
continued to describe his maneuver as an intelligent one, and
we may describe the driver as an intelligent driver on the basis
of such evidence. Why, then, is it peculiar to describe a
machine as intelligent?

There seems to be an element of *intention* present in what
the driver does which is necessarily absent from what machines do. However "automatic" our actions become, so long as
they are not mere reflexes, we may assume an element of intention if the action achieves a purpose and is not merely a matter
of luck. "Intention" here does not mean that the driver was in

any way thinking of what he was doing. All that is meant is that the driver *did* get out of his skid and that he wanted to get out of it. His success in achieving this purpose, even though he did not think about it, is evidence of his intention. On the other hand, a machine can be successful at anything from baking pies to proving the theory of relativity without our ever inferring that it "intends" or "wants" to bake pies or prove the theory.

Our conclusion is that routine performances carried out by human beings may be said to be "stupid" or "intelligent" and may be evidence of intelligence or stupidity in the agent. When human beings perform routines they need not be carried out unintentionally, though they may be carried out unthinkingly. This, then, is the minimal criterion for saying that a performance is "intelligent"—that it achieves a purpose which the agent may be said to have intended to achieve and that there is a degree of skill involved in thus achieving it.[16]

(iii) *"Intelligence" as "the ability to learn."*

If any one thing is of the essence of intelligence, if any one thing distinguishes the bright boy from the dunce, it is the ability of the former to pick things up quickly. The ability to learn can, of course, only be tested by testing performances, what has been learnt; but tests of attainment can be, though they need not be, also tests of the ability to learn, and it is only when they are that they can properly be called intelligence tests.[17]

Nowell-Smith maintains that it is "intelligence" in the sense of "the ability to learn" which is tested by intelligence tests. And as he points out, this is not acknowledged by psychologists who devise the tests. Vernon, for example, offers three senses of "intelligence":

(a) The underlying inborn potentiality, that is some quality of the central nervous system, determined ultimately by the genes.

---

[16] It may not always be necessary for the purpose to be actually achieved for us to say that the performance is "intelligent." An "intelligent" solution to a problem need not always be the correct one.

[17] P. H. Nowell-Smith, *The Aristotelian Society Proceedings*, Sup. Vol. XXIV, 1960, p. 97.

(b) The all-round ability or mental efficiency that children or adults actually display in everyday life at school or at work.

(c) The Intelligence Quotient as technically defined.[18]

Intelligence in this third sense is directly tested, but the important question is, "Of what is it a measure?" "With what non-technical sense of intelligence is it roughly correlated?" Vernon denies that I.Q. is a measure of inborn intelligence as opposed to acquired knowledge. He says that we have no means of testing inborn intelligence, which is a "purely hypothetical quality." Rather, I.Q. correlates closely with intelligence in everyday life—this is what makes intelligence tests useful in practice. And Nowell-Smith agrees that someone's actual performance at school or at work depends on such traffic with the actual world as they have had, whatever inborn capacities they may have started with.

However Nowell-Smith points out that there *is* an inborn capacity which intelligence tests seek to measure—the ability to learn. Leaving aside for the moment what he means by "the ability to learn," what does he mean by "inborn?" A capacity may quite properly be said to be inborn. Nowell-Smith's example is the capacity to learn a language, which is inborn in children but not in animals. He makes a crucial distinction between the capacity to *learn*, say, a language and the capacity to *use* it. It is obviously false that a child's capacity to *use* a language is inborn. His actual efficiency in speaking will depend entirely on the environment stimuli. If he does not come into contact with language users he will never learn to speak a language, but his ability to learn it is innately there.

How does Nowell-Smith support his thesis that intelligence tests measure such an innate capacity to learn? He employs two main lines of argument.

(a) The first argument is based on the way the chronological age of the subject being tested enters into the determination of his I.Q. score. I.Q. is *not* directly correlated with actual all-round ability or efficiency of performance. If it were,

18 Nowell-Smith, op. cit., pp. 105–06.

chronological age would not enter into the determination of the intelligence quotient. But the subject's test score, his actual performance, is divided by his chronological age (and multiplied by 100 to eliminate fractions). The tester is not merely measuring the child's present efficiency of performance. A younger child with the same actual performance as an older child is held to have a higher I.Q. The younger child differs from the older child in that he has taken a shorter time to reach the same level of performance. Therefore, I.Q. is a measure of not merely *what* a subject has learned but his *capacity* to learn. This accords with the actual use of I.Q. tests as selection criteria for different types of schooling, "for clearly what we want to know, especially about young children, is not just the extent of their accomplishments, but the *educability* which these accomplishments show."[19]

(b) The other main line of argument which Nowell-Smith advances to support his contention that I.Q. tests are designed to measure innate ability to learn is based on the characteristic attempt of test constructors to eliminate environmental factors (such as parental attitudes, emotional disturbances, social background and so on) from determining the outcome of the tests. The attempt is to test a child's capacity to spot relations quickly and accurately, not to test the range of his vocabulary or knowledge. In fact, the simplicity of the tests is due to the attempt to put the questions within the *knowledge* of a child from any background.

These two arguments make a devastating case against Vernon's view that intelligence tests are not tests of innate ability. How are we to explain Vernon's apparent blindness to such obvious characteristics of intelligence tests? Nowell-Smith identifies Vernon's confusion as being rooted in the idea that we have no means of *assessing* inborn intelligence because we have no means of *observing* it. Vernon seems to think that only when we can observe it can we assess it. Nowell-Smith suggests that this rests on a confusion between (a) a capacity, and (b) the physical characteristics that a thing must have if it has the capacity. He points out that you don't test a car's

[19] Nowell-Smith, op. cit., p. 108.

capacity to do 50 m.p.h. by looking under the hood; you observe its performance. Similarly, you don't need to investigate his brain or nervous system to assess a person's capacities.

It is important to note, in conclusion, that Nowell-Smith's arguments only establish that intelligence tests *seek* to measure innate ability. Sociological critics object that test results are seriously affected by a wide variety of environmental factors, particularly social background. A good example of this sort of criticism may be found in Basil Bernstein's article, "Social Class and Linguistic Development: A Theory of Social Learning."[20]

(iv) *Intelligence tests and education.* It is often taken for granted, even by sociologists, that intelligence tests are the most effective means available of determining those who are capable of higher education. It is important to see that our analysis of "intelligence" as "the ability to learn" is at odds with this assumption. On our analysis, a low I.Q. score indicates a low capacity to learn and a high I.Q. score indicates a high capacity to learn. But a score would need to be very low for us to assume that someone was *incapable* of profiting from higher education. Mark Fisher puts the point plainly:

> If we really cannot afford to provide *every* child with the whole range of learning opportunities available to *any* child, let us be clear that it is poverty which prevents us, and not imagine that we have good reasons.[21]

This is rather an overstatement because the fact that we cannot afford to give such opportunities to children with low learning capacities is a good practical reason. But Fisher is right to insist that we ought to understand that it is poverty which prevents us, not the incapacity of the children. He points out that we never employ tests of capacity to *select* some children for teaching in reading, talking, walking, writing and counting. If a child is abnormal in ways which make it very difficult for him to learn these skills we give him remedial treatment—the tests employed are not designed to *disbar* children from learn-

[20] In *Education, Economy and Society,* ed. A. H. Halsey et al. (London: Collier-Macmillan, Ltd.; New York: The Free Press, 1961) pp. 288–314.
[21] "Intelligence," *Proceedings of the Philosophy of Education Society of Great Britain,* 1966, p. 60.

ing the skills but to identify those who need special treatment. In fact we may well be persuaded that in such cases more resources ought to be devoted to children with low capacities so that they may learn these basic skills. But on what grounds do we distinguish basic skills from those which are not basic? As Fisher puts it:

> Is it *just* because walking, reading, and counting are so important that everyone needs them? Compare these with, for example, singing, painting, writing sonnets, proving algebraic theorems. I think the difference is that we believe that everyone wants, and is right to want because he needs, to walk, write and count. But the same is not conversely conceded of singing, painting and the rest.[22]

We are not denying, of course, that people are right in thinking that there is a "need" to try to teach children to walk, write and count even if this is a very expensive process when the children are abnormal. But we have already observed that reference to needs offers us no way of discriminating what is *not* needed. If we concede that children with a low capacity to learn basic skills ought to receive remedial treatment, on what grounds do we deny remedial treatment to children with a low capacity for higher level activities? This question is one which will figure prominently when we examine the notion of "equality of opportunity" in education. All we can do at present is clear the decks for that discussion by denying that selection by means of intelligence tests is a way of detecting those who are *incapable* of higher education. All the tests can do is to separate those with high capacity for learning from those with low capacity. The high correlation between performance on an I.Q. test and later performance at school or college only holds so long as we do not introduce systematically differential treatment for those with low capacity. If education is a race where everyone receives more or less the same treatment then those with high capacity will undoubtedly be the most successful. If education were run as a "weight-for-ability" race, if those with low capacity were to receive special treatment, the correlation

[22] Ibid.

between performance on an I.Q. test and later performance at school or college would become less and less significant. When we consider "equality of opportunity" in education we will draw attention to the very great difficulties involved in arguing for the distribution of a higher proportion of available resources to the education of the less able. But it is an argument which must be examined, not dismissed on the false assumption that intelligence tests sort out those who are incapable of learning.

(D) CREATIVITY AND EDUCATION°

If we look at an intelligence test we find rather peculiar sorts of questions such as this:

Which two of the following statements most nearly mean the same?

(1) Repentance is poor consolation.

(2) More haste, less speed.

(3) Quick decisions often breed regret.

(4) He'll have a bucket of tears for a cup of joy.

(5) Marry in haste, repent at leisure.

If we ask whether such questions are tests of what is ordinarily called intelligence, we find that psychologists are generally not interested in our question. In order to support their claim that intelligence tests measure intelligence (if they make this claim at all) psychologists point to the correlation between performance on the test and later performance at school or college. While we would sometimes want to distinguish the successful man from the intelligent man, one of the criteria we customarily use to determine whether someone is intelligent is his success at intellectual activities. As it happens there are not particularly good correlations between performances on intelligence tests and later intellectual performances, particularly

° I am indebted to Mr. J. P. White whose paper on Creativity, read to the Philosophy of Education Society of Great Britain, first stimulated my interest in this topic and who was also helpful in referring me to some useful source material on the subject.

when the tests are administered later in school life. Thus, for example, Sixth Form examination results are better predictors of performance at the university than an intelligence test taken at the time of the examination. Of course it *need* not follow that a good correlation between performance on intelligence tests and later performance in activities which do manifestly require intelligence, necessarily implies that the intelligence test measures intelligence. It may test something *else* which correlates highly with later accomplishment in intellectual spheres. Thus, for example, British sociologists (such as Bernstein, op. cit.) maintain that part of the reason for the high correlation between intelligence tests taken at eleven years of age and later performance is that the test discriminates in favor of middle-class children. They argue that the tests are partially tests of middle-class vocabulary and modes of thought. And since for obvious reasons middle-class children are more likely to be encouraged to go to college and to do well than are lower-class children, the tests are not merely tests of intelligence but of a number of other factors as well.

While the claim that intelligence tests measure intelligence may be vulnerable on grounds such as these, there is at least *some* evidence that there are *some* sorts of connections between performances of the kind which we ordinarily call intelligent and odd performances such as deciding whether or not "carpentry is to furniture as heat is to ashes" or working out the code for PAT if BOARD is written LQDVI in the code. Whether such performances are connected with intelligence or not, most psychologists agree that the important thing is that high scores on the tests are predictive of intelligent performance at school or college. If there were no such correlation then presumably there would be no grounds for claiming that they are tests of intelligence as we usually understand it.

The first thing to notice about creativity tests is that there has been no attempt to establish that success in the test is predictive of creativity in other fields. If it could be shown that success in answering a question like, "How many uses can you think of for a brick?" correlated with writing good poetry, painting good pictures, composing good music or evolving fruitful scientific hypotheses, we might be led to agree that the tests actually did test the "ability to create." But *no* such correlations have been established. In fact the little work that has been done on people who are creative in such varied spheres suggests that there is very little connection between high scores on creativity tests and actually being highly creative.[23] The claim that the tests measure creativity rests on the assumption that answers to the questions on the tests are themselves evidence of creativity. And this we shall staunchly deny.

Consider, for example, some items from tests used by J. P. Guilford, of the University of Southern California, in twenty years of testing what Americans call "high-grade adults" for creative ability:

* Write down as many unusual uses as possible for a brick.
* Write down as many words ending in "*-tion*" as possible, regardless of meaning.
* Give as many descriptions of a parcel as possible.

It is very difficult to see how such items could test creative ability. The main criterion for creativity according to such tests is merely a *quantitative* one. The more answers given, the more creative you are supposed to be. It is true that we sometimes relate creativity to quantity of production. In this sense Shakespeare was a more creative writer than Emily Brontë, and Picasso a more creative painter than da Vinci. It must, however, be observed that we only relate creativity to quantity of production when the *quality* of what is being produced is of a high standard. Thus we would not maintain that Georgette Heyer is more creative than Emily Brontë, despite the huge output of the former and the tiny production of the latter.

There is a point here which is of great importance for the teaching of creative writing and of art. The lack of concern on the part of some teachers of art and writing for the *quality* of children's paintings and writings is closely related to the educational psychologist's lack of concern with, or ignorance of, the importance of qualitative considerations in teaching art

[23] See, for example, Liam Hudson, *Contrary Imaginations* (London: Methuen & Co., Ltd., 1966) p. 107.

and writing. There are a large number of books which point out to teachers that children's art and composition is often an attempt to deal symbolically with difficulties in their relations with parents, brothers, sisters, friends. There can be no doubt that children's art is often an attempt to deal with personal problems. Unfortunately, it is sometimes suggested in books for teachers of English and art that the teacher should see his function as a therapeutic one. He should, according to this account, be primarily concerned with helping children come to terms with their personal problems through their attempts to symbolically order their experience. But as we have already argued in this chapter, the educator is not some sort of doctor; he is not concerned with *curing* his pupils. The standards which apply to the teaching of art and English are not standards which relate to personal adjustment and mental health. They are standards which relate to what is good or bad painting or good or bad writing. If a teacher feels that a child's mental health will be impaired unless he is allowed to work out his problems in painting or poetry, the teacher may have an obligation to let the child do so. But this is surely an exceptional situation, and, as we have suggested before, it would surely be preferable if such cases were passed on to qualified psychologists.

The influence of psychology of the "creativity testing" sort and of the "therapeutic" sort has had a deleterious effect on the teaching of art and writing because of the total failure of psychologists to grasp or even consider what worthwhile work in art or English would be like. This disregard for qualitative standards in teaching these subjects has seeped even into parental attitudes as exemplified by a story in the English *Times Educational Supplement:*

> The place is the kitchen of a suburban ranch house near Chicago. The time is ten past noon. A solemn five-year-old marches in. Wordless, he hands his mother a huge sheet of paper, half covered with vague shapes in grey. "Oh, darling", says she, "how wonderful. What subtle colours. I think it's the nicest picture you ever made. I like the feel of it . . . the way you use the space over here . . . it's

very interesting." At this point, the young man, who had
listened in stony silence, interrupted her. "It isn't," he said
disdainfully, "it fell in the mud." Then he turned on his
heel and left the scene of a letdown.

The *Times* correspondent wonders how the mother would have
reacted if her son had brought home a kelly green triangle with
a many-pointed yellow thing on the tip and proclaimed it a
Christmas tree. Perhaps a polite "Very nice dear" and then an
aside to us, "It looks exactly like twenty-five other Christmas
trees" and (sigh) "When he was little he used to have this
marvelous freedom. I don't know what's happened to the child.
His pictures have become so conventional."

"Conventional"—this is the term which is so frequently
opposed to "creative," "imaginative," "original" by those who
have no notion of the relationship between convention and
originality in art or literature. For them, if a story or painting is
unusual or different it is original or imaginative. The hard,
disciplined work which so many artists and writers go through
in order to master by imitation the techniques of writers and
painters who have preceded them is often disregarded. In
so many cases, however, the conventional is the basis for
original and creative work and forms a major part of it. (It
is harder to find exceptions to this generalization than to find
examples, but Pope's poetry is a very good example. The
heroic couplet and conventional verse forms give Pope's poetry
the measured assurance and order which his poems praise. At
the same time Pope invests these conventional forms with a
flexibility of movement and an easy wit which make him the
most original poet of the eighteenth century.)

J. W. Getzels, and P. W. Jackson in *Creativity and Intelligence* are particularly given to describing any unusual or
unconventional remarks that a child may make as creative.
Nonconformity, rebelliousness or just plain silly nonsense in
what the children write or draw is solemnly taken as evidence
of creativity. So often the so-called "high creatives" are highly
conforming—they conform to non-conformism. They are, in
the children's own terms, "professional knockers." What could

be more conventional, in the tradition of Holden Caulfield (in Salinger's *Catcher in the Rye*) and the "angry generation," than this response to a picture of a boy, from an allegedly high creative subject. He writes:

> The boy's name is Jack Evans and he is a senior in school who gets C's and B's, hates soccer, does not revolt against convention and has a girl friend named Lois who is a typical sorority fake. He is studying when someone entered the room who he likes. He has a dull life in terms of anything that is not average. His parents are pleased because they have a red-blooded American boy. Actually he is horribly average. He will go to college, take over his Dad's business, marry the girl and do absolutely nothing in the long run.[24]

Getzels and Jackson are particularly fond of this example. They come back to it later (p. 105) as evidencing the high-creative adolescent's "other-centered" or disinterested social criticism, his debunking of conventional form and stereotyped ideals. They cite in particular such phrases as "typical sorority fake" and "red-blooded American boy." If they listened to children in the streets and playground they would have realized that almost any adolescent schoolboy conversation will have, as its conventional mode, rubbishing of this sort. It is evidence not of creativity, but of a facile, readily available stock response.

Similarly, Getzels and Jackson have little hesitation in describing that which is fanciful, fantastic or dreamlike as creative. Such an assumption is a most common error of psychologists when they speak of creativity in the arts, or, indeed, in the sciences or in history, and it is only possible so long as there is complete ignorance or lack of concern with the distinction between good and bad works of art and good and bad scientific or historical hypotheses. Since it is notoriously difficult to convince those who are not literary critics that there is a significant difference between genuinely creative or imaginative works and the work of children or neurotics we will

[24] J. W. Getzels and P. W. Jackson, *Creativity and Intelligence* (New York: John Wiley & Sons, Inc., 1962) p. 41.

develop this point with reference to creativity or imagination in science or history. We would surely not credit anyone as being creative or imaginative in science or history if they never produced hypotheses which were *good* ones. Of the myriad scientific hypotheses which have been evolved, it is mainly the ones that work, or at least look as if they will work, which earn the accolade "creative" or "imaginative" for the originator. This reflects that these terms imply some measure of quality or worth in the ideas put forward. And although this is true of artistic creation as well it would require a detailed argument to establish that there are criteria for judging art to be good or bad. Since this would lead us too far from our main concerns we could put the point conditionally. *If* there are such criteria in estimating the quality of works of art, then creative, original or imaginative art is that which is good art. We do not describe artistic failures in these terms, for they are terms of approbation. If we want fantasy or mere difference or newness, then we can go to science fiction and some of the excesses of modern painting and sculpture.

These considerations lead us to reject Getzels and Jackson's frequent identification of creativity with the production of what is merely off-beat, different, fantastic or amusing. The world of the high creative which Getzels and Jackson describe on the basis of autobiographies written by those who do well on creativity tests is, they say

> a world of fantasy . . . It is a world that may be entered to escape the mundane, the pedestrian, and the trivial aspects of reality—a secret chamber providing solace to the Walter Mitty in everyone—but it is also a world containing the shock of the unexpectedly grotesque, a carnival funny house in which daydream may be transformed into nightmare.[25]

When Getzels and Jackson quote some bad verse by E. E. Cummings,[26] which sentimentalizes the alleged courage of the

[25] Ibid., p. 105.
[26] Ibid., p. 106.
"The poet is one who is prepared to
Carve immortal jungles of despair
To hold a mountain's heartbeat in his hand."

creative artist, they add that they are not suggesting that their high creatives, with their "little inventions and unformed fantasies" are exhibiting anything like the courage Cummings is talking about. But they cannot help wondering, they say, whether if properly nourished out of such childish forays— "with their prizes of 'skid-proof face cream,' ' . . . cereal that bends, sags and sways'—a grander type of valor might be born."[27]

This nonsense about "valor" has nothing to do with the issue. The significant admission is that the best of what the high creatives actually produce in response to the creativity tests are "little inventions and unformed fantasies." What Getzels and Jackson ought to be wondering, before the words "creative," "imaginative" and "original" appear in the pages of their book, is not whether a grander type of valor might be born, whatever that is, but whether anything creative, original or imaginative has been or will be produced by children who have shown only that they can produce little inventions and unformed fantasies. We do not find out from Getzels and Jackson, despite all their elaborate investigations, whether or not the allegedly high creative children have written good stories, painted good paintings, produced good musical compositions or put forward good hypotheses in science or history classes.

It is to Liam Hudson's credit that in his book *Contrary Imaginations* he points out that there is scarcely a shred of evidence to support the view that open-ended tests of the sort which he uses in his own investigations and which are used by Getzels and Jackson are tests of creativity. Instead, he refers to them as tests of "divergent thinking" and refers to intelligence tests as tests of "convergent thinking." In an intelligence test the individual is set a problem to which he is required to find the right answer—there is one solution and the individual's reasoning may be said to "converge" on the right answer. Whereas in the so-called creativity test, the individual is invited to "diverge," to think fluently and tangentially, without examining any one line of reasoning in detail; thus there are thousands of

[27] Ibid.

possible uses for a brick. Just what the criteria are for deciding that one answer is more ingenious or witty than another is not clear, but it is at least preferable that testers profess to be testing these qualities, rather than creativity, originality, or imagination.

Much of our argument in this section relates in an important way to our earlier analysis of the nature of "ability." We often hear English teachers and art teachers say, when they are asked why they teach these subjects, that they are developing or training the children's "imagination" or their "creative ability." But "the imagination" is a mythical beast. We can teach children, with varying degrees of success, to write stories, paint pictures, compose musical pieces which are to varying degrees imaginative or creative. ("Teaching" here would probably not involve much "telling," though there are many things we *can* tell children about how to write and how to paint.) The point is that we do not try to get children to think up scientific hypotheses or put themselves in the shoes of historical personages or paint pictures *in order to* develop their creativity or their imaginative ability. For what we *mean* by developing creativity or imaginative ability is getting them to perform these varied tasks as well as they are able. Furthermore when we are getting a child to paint good pictures we are not developing the *same* capacity as we are when we're getting him to write good poems. Proficiency at one thing may be and often is accompanied by incompetence at another. (William Blake is the only great English poet who is also a considerable painter. Lawrence was a pretty awful painter and Turner a rather peculiar poet.)

If we *mean* by developing a child's "imaginative capacity" we are getting him to paint good pictures, write good poems and so on, it follows that it is quite unilluminating to speak of the development of imagination or creativity as the *aim* of teaching these skills. It is merely a misleading way of referring to their intrinsic value, just as speaking of the development of intellect as an aim of education is a way of referring to the intrinsic value of the development of understanding.

The main points which have been made in this section are as follows:

1. There has been no attempt of the sort which has been made with intelligence tests to correlate performances on creativity tests with creative performances outside the tests. So that if the tests are to be tests of creativity, the actual answers to test items must evidence creativity.

2. Creativity test questions are designed mainly to measure quantity of work rather than quality of work. But since the decisive factor in referring to a piece of work as creative is its quality, the tests fail in this respect to discriminate what is creative from what is not.

3. In so far as creativity testers also attempt to make qualitative distinctions they fail miserably. They confuse that which is merely unconventional, fanciful or amusing with that which is creative, original or imaginative. The tests provide very little opportunity for creative work.

4. There need be no connection between being creative or imaginative in one field and being creative or imaginative in another.

5. It is misleading to refer to the development of creativity or imagination as an aim of teaching people anything. If we teach people to write imaginative poems or paint imaginative pictures or solve imaginative scientific hypotheses then this is *all* we are doing. There is no general ability or mental muscle that we are exercising or developing when we do each of these things.

SECTION (A)

Basic References

BANTOCK, G. H. "The School and Mental Health," *Education, Culture and the Emotions*. London: Faber and Faber, Ltd., 1967.

PETERS, R. S., " 'Mental Health' as an Educational Aim," *Aims in Education*, ed. T. H. B. Hollins. Manchester, England: Manchester University Press, 1964.

———, *Authority, Responsibility and Education*, Chapter 4. London: Allen & Unwin, Ltd., 1963.

————, "Education as Initiation," in *Philosophical Analysis and Education,* ed. R. D. Archambault. London: Routledge and Kegan Paul, Ltd., 1965.

Further References

DEWEY, JOHN, *Experience and Education*

————, *The Child and the Curriculum*

SCHEFFLER, I., *The Language of Education,* Chapter 3.

Essay/Discussion Topics

* The combination of sexual maturity and occupational immaturity extending over a decade of vigorous youthful life is all but intentionally designed to violate the most fundamental precepts of mental hygiene. Early marriage is the solution that seems best to conserve all the biological and social values involved, but only a fortunate few appear to be able to arrange for this preferred response. Contraceptive devices are now widely understood and there is little doubt that they have encouraged temporary and experimental unions, the usefulness of which is still uncertain. Deliberate promiscuity on the part of either sex is abnormal, at least in the statistical sense, and usually points to some personality barrier to genuine happiness. Homosexuality is a clinical puzzle in itself, but also a sample of the need for tolerance in appraising many of the inferior modes of sexual adjustment into which individuals fall when their normal emotional development is hampered. Psychologists have no *a priori* right to insist that life-long monogamous marriages are the only happy ones conceivable, but matched against the alternatives commonly attempted, it comes out distinctly in first place. Under these circumstances, it seems but proper that our educational program should be directed toward making this form of family organization as successful as possible by building attitudes and controls early in life favourable to this outcome. (George W. Hartmann, *Educational Psychology* [New York: American Book Co., 1941] pp. 248–49.)

Analyze this passage in detail with reference to the arguments advanced in Section (A).

* Both Peters and Scheffler discuss the use of the "growth" metaphor in education. But neither are basically concerned to analyze Dewey's use of the term. To what extent are their remarks applicable to what Dewey says about "growth"?

SECTION (B)

Basic References

KOMISAR, B. P., "Needs and the Needs Curriculum," *Language and Concepts in Education*, ed. B. O. Smith and R. H. Ennis. Skokie, Illinois: Rand McNally and Co., 1962.

PETERS, R. S., *Ethics and Education*, Chapter VI. London: Allen & Unwin Ltd., 1966.

Further References

FLEMING, C. M., *Teaching: A Psychological Analysis*.

PRESSEY, ROBINSON, AND HORROCKS, *Psychology in Education*, partic. pp. 206–209.

Essay/Discussion Topics

* Depending upon the way "need" is interpreted, the needs-policy turns out to be sometimes trivial, sometimes indeterminate, and sometimes unsupported, but always unimportant. (B. P. Komisar, "Needs and the . . . ," *Language and Concepts in Education*, p. 38)

Discuss.

* How are "needs" related to "interests" and "wants"? Should a curriculum builder take the "interests" or "wants" of children into account?

SECTION (C)

Basic References

MACINTYRE, A. AND NOWELL-SMITH, P. N., "Purposes and Intelligent Actions," *Proceedings of the Aristotelian Society*, supp. vol. 34, partic. pp. 97–112, 1960.

RYLE, G., "Knowing How and Knowing That," *Philosophy and Education*, 2d edition. Scheffler, I., ed. Boston: Allyn and Bacon, Inc., 1966.

WISEMAN, S. (ed.), *Intelligence and Ability*.

Further References

FISHER, M., "Intelligence," *The Proceedings of the Philosophy of Education Society of Great Britain,* 1966.

Essay/Discussion Topics

* "Intelligence is what intelligence tests measure."
Discuss.

* Before there can be intelligent behaviour there must be some purpose to be achieved (though it may be a very general and vague purpose and only become clearer as the events succeed one another), and the behaviour has to have the appearance of being directed towards that end in such a way as to achieve it as quickly, as economically, as cleanly as possible. (G. Thomson, "Intelligence and Civilization," *Intelligence and Ability,* p. 117)

Discuss.

* I have asked myself . . . whether we are doing the right thing both for the individual and the community when we thus take pains, through the medium of our educational system, to direct children of differing degrees of intelligence into different types of school. (G. Thomson, "Intelligence and Civilization," *Intelligence and Ability,* p. 116)

What do you think?

SECTION (D)

Basic References

GETZELS, J. W. AND JACKSON, P. W., *Creativity and Intelligence,* New York: John Wiley & Sons, Inc., 1962.

HUDSON, L., *Contrary Imaginations,* partic. chap. 6. London: Methuen & Co., Ltd., 1966.

VERNON, P. E., "Creativity and Intelligence," *Educational Research,* Vol. vi, No. 3, June, 1964.

Further References

KOESTLER, A., *The Act of Creation.*

Essay/Discussion Topics

* Can one distinguish between creative and intelligent children?

> * Nothing, I am convinced, so roundly condemns its owner as the belief that originality is a simple affair . . . However much we may complain to the contrary, psychology remains a discipline with practical influence—through the beliefs of parents, teachers and administrators—over the shaping of children's lives. It follows that our over-simplifications may be translated into practical blunders. (Liam Hudson, *Contrary Imaginations*, pp. 121–122)

In what ways could over-simplifications about "creativity" be translated into practical blunders?

Do you know of any other over-simplifications in the educational psychology you have read which could become practical blunders?

* What would be the criteria for being "creative" or "original" in a particular art form or discipline with which you are familiar?

5

Morality
and
Education

(A) PSYCHOLOGICAL DETERMINISM
AND RESPONSIBILITY

WE HAVE BEEN CRITICAL of a trend in educational psychology which suggests that teachers ought to be primarily engaged in various sorts of therapeutic or remedial work with children. An overriding preoccupation with "mental health," for example, frequently involves the assumption that people in general, and children in particular, are not really responsible for what they do and say. Instead, they are viewed as being subject to various sorts of psychological and social pressures which determine what they do and say. Most of us have experienced the strength of peer group pressures, for example, in our own school days most of us can remember having broken school rules because this was a way of "proving ourselves" to the group. We are probably less aware of pressures which stem from our early upbringing which lead us to do one thing rather than another. But if it is the case that our actions are determined in such ways, to the extent that we could not in general be said to be responsible for what we do, there would be little point in going on to discuss moral education or punishment. Instead, we would presumably go on to talk in such manipulative terms as "adjustment," "therapy," "building in preferred responses," "integration" and so on. Since we intend to abjure such terms as these and to talk instead about moral education, our first task is to give full consideration to the case for psychological determinism insofar as it works against the view that people are generally responsible.

The arguments for psychological determinism take two main forms which we shall classify as "strong" and "weak." In its strong form, the contention is that whatever reasons a man gives for his actions, there will always be a further explanation for the fact that these reasons weighed with him rather than others. This further explanation is said to be the real explanation of the actions, for it is this further explanation which indicates what "causes" him to perform the actions and to adopt the reasons he gives for them. In its weak form, the argument can hardly be said to be a determinist one. The claim is made that many, even all, of the assessments we make of our motives and reasons for acting are at best incomplete or partial. Reasons or motives of which we are unaware or unconscious may operate in addition to our acknowledged reasons and in some cases cause us to adopt the reasons we acknowledge. This is quite different from the strong determinist argument, for this is the claim that behind our acknowledged reasons for acting there are *always* factors of which the agent is usually unaware which cause him to do what he does and give the reasons he does.

The strong determinist position is often implicit in what psychologists say and it has actually been made quite explicit and supported by an otherwise sound philosopher, John Hospers. We will give his argument detailed consideration. He offers the following account of the "wider acceptance" of psychological determinism in the twentieth century:

> Heretofore it was pretty generally thought that while we could not rightly blame a person for the color of his eyes or the morality of his parents, or even for what he did at the age of three, or to a large extent what impulses he had or whom he fell in love with, one *could* do so for other of his

adult activities, particularly the acts he performed voluntarily and with premeditation. Later this attitude was shaken. Many voluntary acts came to be recognized, at least in some circles, as compelled by the unconscious. Some philosophers recognized this too—Ayer (1946) talks about the kleptomaniac being unfree, and about a person being unfree when another person exerts an habitual ascendancy over his personality. But this is as far as he goes. The usual examples, such as the kleptomaniac and the schizophrenic, apparently satisfy most philosophers, and with these exceptions removed, the rest of mankind is permitted to wander in the vast and alluring fields of freedom and responsibility. So far, the inroads upon freedom left the vast majority of humanity untouched; they began to hit home when the psychiatrists began to realize, though philosophers did not, that the domination of the conscious by the unconscious extended, not merely to a few exceptional individuals, but to all human beings, that the "big three behind the scenes" [a reference to the "id," the "super-ego" and the "ego," about which more in a moment] are not respecters of persons, and dominate us all, even including the *sanctum sanctorum* of freedom our conscious will. To be sure, the domination by the unconscious in the case of "normal" individuals is somewhat more benevolent than the tyranny and despotism exercised in neurotic cases, and because the former have evoked less comment; but the principle remains in all cases the same: the unconscious is the master of every fate and the captain of every soul.[1]

Despite the rhetorical flourishes here and there, this is a straightforward statement of the position we are calling strong psychological determinism. In the following extract from the conclusion of the article there is a slight weakening, but the vast range of actions, dispositions and decisions which Hospers claims are unconsciously determined or compelled is worth recording:

. . . most human behavior cannot be called free at all: our impulses and volitions having to do with our basic attitude

[1] From *Readings in Ethical Theory,* selected and edited by Wilfred Sellars and John Hospers, p. 572. © 1952. Reprinted by permission of Appleton-Century-Crofts, Division of Meredith Corporation.

towards life, whether we are optimists or pessimists, tough-minded or tender-minded, whether our tempers are quick or slow, whether we are "naturally self-seeking" or "naturally benevolent" (*and all the acts consequent upon these things*), what things annoy us, whether we take to blondes or brunettes, old or young, whether we become artists or philosophers or businessmen—all this has its basis in the unconscious. If people generally call most acts free, it is not because they believe that compelled acts should be called free, it is rather through not knowing how large a proportion of our acts actually are compelled.[2]

How does Hospers illustrate his argument? He has some exotic cases from psychoanalytic case studies, but the only way of disputing them would be to tackle the whole explanatory apparatus of psychoanalysis (which is by no means secure in its theoretical foundations). The really important test for strong determinism is whether or not "normal" actions by "normal" people can be shown to be "compelled by the unconscious." Hospers proposes that we leave aside the question of how clearly and on what grounds one can distinguish the neurotic from the normal and offers as an illustration a proclivity that everyone would call normal—namely the decision of a man to support his wife and possibly a family. Hospers describes the genesis of such a decision according to psychoanalytic accounts. The passage is cited in full (pp. 142–145) as the first topic for discussion at the end of this chapter, since it is representative of a wide range of strong determinist arguments. We cannot hope to do justice to the whole range, but we ought at least to consider one case in detail.

    Let us accept for the purposes of argument that in certain circumstances it makes sense to employ such concepts as "face-saving," "identification," "ego" and so on in explaining why people behave as they do. Take the autarchic fiction, for example, and the idea that it is shattered during weaning. What leads the psychoanalyst to maintain that children's behavior may be explained, in certain respects, by assuming that children have an omnipotence complex, or illusion of nondepen-

2 Ibid., p. 575.

dence? As Hospers suggests, it is the odd behavior of the child during weaning—the child's reaction is "anger and fury; and he responds by kicking and biting etc." Hence the explanation "the shattering of the autarchic fiction is a great disillusionment to every child, a tremendous blow to his ego which he will, in one way or another, spend the rest of his life trying to repair."[3] Leaving aside the reference to later life, we could agree that childish tantrums do seem to require some hypothesis of the sort which the psychoanalyst offers, for they do not seem to be justified by the apparently small changes of routine the child undergoes. A similar reference to oddness of behavior underlies Hospers claim that a man acts out in later life his repressed feelings against his mother—he refers to the "constant deprecation for women's duties"—"All she does is stay home and get together a few meals and she calls that work." If a man were to constantly deprecate women's work in such ways, we might begin to think that his actions were related to unfortunate childhood experiences. Hospers' culminating contention, that a man provides for his wife and family as a face-saving device, to deny his early dependence which is so embarrassing to his ego, is related to the assumption that a man generally dislikes to be reminded of his babyhood when he was dependent on women. Once again, we may be inclined to resort to stories of early dependence if a man's reactions to such reminders were extreme—if he tears up old photos of himself in his mother's arms, snubs his great-aunts, and when his old rocking-horse is discovered in the attic, he makes a bonfire of it. And if, on such occasions he is aggressively domineering towards his wife, we might even say that his "choice" of a wife had something to do with "face-saving" as Hospers maintains.

Hospers' account of the unconscious motivation which leads to a man's decision to support a wife and family is open to numerous objections but we are attempting to isolate the fundamental one. Stories about the unconscious are only plausible if they are related to *peculiarities* in someone's behavior which cannot otherwise be explained. Although Hospers

[3] Ibid., p. 569.

claims to be explaining a normal choice, he recurs constantly to abnormalities in behavior. Without reference to such abnormalities we could quite legitimately accept a man's reasons for his decision to support his family. Hospers does not support the view that when a man makes a decision to support his family on the grounds that he has a moral obligation to do so, his reason can necessarily be shown to be a rationalization for hidden motives stemming from his "unconscious."

The weak form of psychological determinism is more plausible, but the important question is whether it could be said to be a determinist argument. J. F. Thompson, in a discussion with P. F. Strawson, puts the weak form as follows:

> Surely the determinist is not committed to saying that the reasons people give for what they do are never good reasons; but only that whether the reasons they give are good or bad, there will always be a further explanation of the fact that these reasons weighed with them.[4]

He asks Strawson if there is "anything patently absurd in that suggestion." Strawson replies that he doesn't think it is absurd, but he suggests that it is in some danger of turning out to be rather trivial:

> As the thesis stands, it contains too many blank cheques, so to speak, for one to be sure what it amounts to. We have to ask, surely, what kind of "further explanation" is envisaged here. For example, if someone has, and avows, a perfectly good reason for something that he does, it is, I suppose, some sort of further explanation of his behaviour to say that he is quite an intelligent person, whose upbringing and present circumstances are perfectly normal and satisfactory, so that he is, in short, a rational man—the sort of man who tends to adopt good reasons as his reasons for doing things. But then two questions arise: first, it seems to me highly doubtful whether a "further explanation" of this kind lends any suport to any thesis that could aptly be called determinism:—the points that add up to his being a

[4] *Freedom and the Will*, ed. D. F. Pears (London: Macmillan and Co., Ltd., 1965) pp. 58–9.

rational man may explain his behaviour, but why should we say that they determine it? And, secondly, surely a "further explanation" to the effect that someone is a rational man has no tendency to undermine the explanation he himself gives of his own behaviour. Just the contrary, in fact; if the reasons he gives are good reasons, the fact that he is a rational man strengthens the view that the good reasons he gives really explain his behaviour.[5]

Strawson is not denying that behind or besides our acknowledged reasons there may lurk unacknowledged reasons, perhaps of a less reputable kind, of which we are wholly or partly unconscious. It may be that behind a man's acknowledged reasons for marrying and supporting his family lie motives of the sort Hospers refers to. But there are no grounds for applying the sort of theory that Hospers advances unless there is some peculiarity or oddity in the reasons the man offers or in the manner he pursues his actions which suggests that further explanation in psychoanalytic terms is required.

Although we may well doubt whether the "weak" form of determinism is a determinist argument at all, it does raise an important point about responsibility. G. J. Warnock, who also participated in the discussion with Thompson and Strawson, describes the weak determinist argument in the way we have presented it but completely misconstrues its relation to questions of responsibility. He says that

> . . . it is hard to see that it offers even a limited support to determinism. When a man is brought to acknowledge an unacknowledged reason as his he certainly sees his action in a different light. But not as an action for which he can disclaim responsibility.[6]

This is a very puzzling remark. An offender who is tortured by guilt and convinced of his responsibility for his crime because his acknowledged reason is an admission of evil intent may surely disclaim responsibility if psychiatric evidence draws his attention to reasons which he had not even recognized himself. Consider, for example, this case cited by Hospers:

[5] Ibid., p. 59.
[6] Ibid., p. 62.

A young man calls at an apartment to make a delivery, rings the bell, talks to the girl who answers the bell, enters the apartment, and stabs her to death with a dozen stabs of an ice pick.[7]

Hospers suggests that our response would be to say, "An unspeakable, foul murder," though few people would be quite so ready to condemn prior to *any* knowledge of motive. "But is it excusable?" asks Hospers. The girl wore a ring which resembled the young man's mother's wedding ring, and when he saw the ring he absolutely could not control himself. Why not?

Because he had revered his mother, and dreamt of her even when she sent him to an orphanage to get rid of him, even when he was pushed around from one orphanage to another and wanted by no one. Then one day when he came to visit his mother unexpectedly, he discovered she was a common whore. He could not take psychologically, this awful ambivalence between hating her for what she was, shattering all his cherished illusions about her, and yet loving her and wanting her desperately as the only anchor in his life, weak as it was. Her wedding ring was the symbol of her sanctity and no one else could wear one in his eyes because it threatened that image of her which he wanted to preserve; yet at the same time he hated her, and the symbol of her sanctity was a mockery of what she really was—when he saw the ring he had to kill.[8]

Clearly this long chain of reasons is not of the sort that the young man would acknowledge to himself. They are unacknowledged reasons which the psychiatrist brings to his attention. The young man may be tortured by guilt for his crime, convinced of his malicious intent, and of his responsibility for committing murder, but when he is made aware of the unacknowledged reasons for his action, he would surely have some case for disclaiming responsibility for the action.

In his *Authority, Responsibility and Education,* R. S. Peters takes a tough line, not unlike Warnock's, on questions of

---

[7] John Hospers, *Human Conduct: An Introduction to the Problems of Ethics* (New York: Harcourt, Brace & World, Inc., 1961) p. 496.

[8] Ibid., p. 496.

responsibility. "To understand all is not necessarily to pardon all," says Peters. But it may be more often than Peters is willing to admit. So many of the judgments which we make about the actions of pupils in classrooms ignore the possibility that the pupils might have psychological problems which, to varying degrees, compel them to behave as they do. It would be unfortunate if our opposition to the view that teachers ought to be primarily concerned with improving the mental health of their pupils were construed as a general cynicism about the possibility that we could have very distressed or disturbed children in our classes. We have already referred to the difficult boy, whom we treated harshly, whose mother said, in front of the child, "We didn't want him in the first place and we still don't want him." The boy's acknowledged reason for misbehaving was (quite explicitly) "Teachers are bastards." But beneath this tough and bitter outer shell we often find a pathetic unacknowledged desire for affection, recognition and understanding. Once this is understood, a lot must be pardoned.

The point is that we are concerned with *children,* and this fact does transform some of the issues concerned with responsibility. We can agree with Peters that

> There is a presumption in favour of *men* being usually responsible for their actions, and the fact that we single out odd cases [e.g., stealing while sleepwalking or by mistake] suggests that we believe that in general men can help doing what they do.[9]

But it is far from clear that this presupposition holds with children. Do we, in general, assume children to be responsible for their actions? We often single out the odd cases who act responsibly and make them house captains or prefects. It is not that being a child is an "exonerating circumstance," like being a schizophrenic or suffering from amnesia. Being a child does not constitute a plea to rebut the assumption of responsibility for it is not at all clear that this assumption holds for children as it does for adults. Of course it may be an effective teaching

[9] R. S. Peters, *Authority, Responsibility and Education* (London: Allen & Unwin, Ltd., 1959) p. 58. Author's italics. Reprinted by permission of Allen & Unwin, Ltd. and Paul S. Eriksson, Inc.

device, in moral education, to act towards children as if you assumed them to be responsible, for this often has the effect that they attempt to live up to your expectations. But one often suspects that teachers who employ this device for a long time actually become convinced that children *are* responsible for what they do in the same way we generally assume adults are. It is well worth keeping your ears open in the school staffroom when children's sexual or excretory behavior draws attention. The assumption often is that the children are deliberately dirty-minded or filthy. There was the case of the boy who carved obscene pictures under his desk lid, whose distinctive style suggested that he was the school's most accomplished lavatory artist. Naturally he paid the penalty for being "dirty"—the assumption that he was fully "responsible" for his actions was unquestioned in the staffroom. Some time after this he brought to the author's class a fine collection of *National Geographic* magazines devoted to pictorial reconstructions of ancient civilizations. Looking through these I found that a number of pages had been cut out or partially removed. The contexts of the pictures suggested that the gaps would have been filled with slave girls in various stages of undress. When asked about this, the boy said that his mother had censored the lot—had laboriously gone through the whole collection with the scissors. In what sense could he be said to be responsible for his preoccupation with naked women?

Peters sometimes gives the unfortunate impression that he is one of the contributors to the sort of staffroom consensus which ought to be resisted. His story of the girl in the remand house who says to the probation officer, "It's no good doing anything for me miss; you see I come from a broken home," has many variants in staffrooms. What could be more apocryphal than the story of the boy who pleaded that he came from a broken home and added, "I broke it." These hoary stories are just as indicative of a reactionary malaise which is opposed to the "progressive malaise" which Peters is attacking. Consider Peters' scoffing attitude toward the "mixed up kid," as he calls him, who according to Peters is an example of the malaise which leads people "to justify, or excuse, their failure to take responsibility for their own lives by an appeal to causes." The "mixed up kid" says that he cannot help trying to strangle his girl friend because his mother rejected him, or preferred his younger brother, or something like that. Perhaps he cannot help it, says Peters—and then adds sceptically—"Perhaps."

Let us consider this example seriously. The dust jacket of *Authority, Responsibility and Education* informs us that Peters was once a youth leader. So let us imagine one of his boys coming up to him and telling him that he can't help trying to strangle his girl friend. Is Peters' reply in the same vein as his comments in his book? Does he say to the boy, "My contention is that there are usually, in fact, very poor grounds for this sort of belief?" Does he suggest to the boy that he is mixed up about Freud as well as about other things? Does he point out that the more strongly he believes he cannot help it, the less likely he will be able to help it and that if he keeps it up, his belief may foster a reality? Surely there are very good grounds for thinking that there is a reality here. Wanting to strangle one's girl friend is a very peculiar thing to want to do. It is almost a paradigm of the sort of case where we do want to drop the talk of responsibility and freewill and rationality and adopt the determinist's descriptions of being compelled to do something.

Given a choice between the malaise which Peters reflects on such occasions and the "contemporary malaise" of which Hospers would be a representative, we find it preferable to err on the side of understanding and sympathy, especially where children and adolescents are concerned. Peters' insistence on the necessity for a "rule of law" in classrooms is good common sense, especially when we are confronted with large classes, overloaded timetables and unruly children. Much of the time we are simply unable to pay much attention to the possibility that a child's unruliness may be caused by factors over which he has no control and which would lead us to say that he was not responsible for his behavior. But it would be very unfortunate if these practical difficulties bred a cynicism about the *desirability* of keeping a lookout for such cases.

In what ways does our contention that children are, in

general, less responsible for what they do and say than are adults affect our views on moral education? There is undoubtedly a close connection between acting responsibly and acting morally, for the notion of *choosing* is fundamental to morality. If children's behavior could always be shown to be determined by forces outside their control, moral education would hardly be a starter. Even in the light of our contention that children are more subject to various sorts of social and psychological determining forces than are adults, it will be plain that the job of the moral educator will not be an easy one. But in some important respects the difficulty here is not one which is peculiar to moral education, but is part of a general educational problem. Getting children to care for standards of truth and beauty is closely connected in a number of ways with getting them to care for moral standards. Many of the determining pressures on children which work against general education work in similar ways against moral education. We will be pointing out that there *is* a difference because moral education involves a marked emphasis on what children do as well as what they think. But these are issues which must be deferred until we consider a matter of prior importance. We must not skid over the very real doubts that exist about whether there is a valid *content* to moral education. No discussion of moral education can begin until we have considered what is involved in making moral judgments.

(B) MORAL JUDGMENTS

If at this point in our discussion, an educational philosopher were to leave his room and walk across his campus to have a word with a moral philosopher, he could well bump into the moral philosopher walking across to have a word with him. This strange meeting could be with Professor R. M. Hare, who has recently proposed that moral philosophers should address themselves to the question, "How should we educate our children?" Let us examine very briefly the background of ethical controversy which has led to Hare's suggestion.

The widespread scepticism about the possibility of finding

common criteria for making moral judgments is to be found in educational philosophy. R. F. Atkinson, for example says:

> Take any moral position and its opposite can be maintained without logical error or factual mistake. It can, of course, be taught and learnt (it is a possible object of knowledge) that a certain moral position is held by certain people, but, whatever adequate grounds for holding a moral position might be, it is clear that this is not among them. There can be moral teaching, instruction in, as opposed to instruction about morality, only if there are criteria of truth, cogency, correctness in the field. Are there such criteria?[10]

Looking around the battleground of modern ethics, Atkinson concludes that no recent moral philosopher has found a way round the point that irreducible differences are possible in morality, that "justifications" in this field have "the remarkable property of failing to exclude opposed alternatives."

This state of affairs stems directly from this observation of David Hume's, made in the mid-eighteenth century:

> In every system of morality, which I have hitherto met with, I have always remark'd, that the author proceeds for some time in the ordinary way of reasoning and establishes the being of a God, or makes observations concerning human affairs; when of a sudden I am surpriz'd to find, that instead of the usual copulations or propositions, *is* and *is not,* I meet with no proposition that is not connected with an *ought,* or an *ought not.* This change is imperceptible; but it is, however, of the last consequence. For as this *ought,* or *ought not,* expresses some new relation or affirmation, 'tis necessary that it shou'd be observed and explain'd; and at the same time that a reason should be given, for what seems altogether inconceivable, how this new relation can be a deduction from others, which are entirely different from it. But as authors do not commonly use this precaution, I shall presume to recommend it to the readers; and am persuaded, that this small attention wou'd subvert

[10] "Instruction and Indoctrination," *Philosophical Analysis and Education,* p. 176.

all the vulgar systems of morality, and let us see that the distinction of vice and virtue is not founded merely on the relations of objects, nor is perceived by reason.[11]

Hume's point is a revolutionary one, for what he is saying is that no moral judgment can be deduced from any set of premises which does not in itself contain a moral judgment or principle. This recognition is fundamentally responsible for the present dilemma in moral philosophy; one's choice of the first premises seems to be an arbitrary matter. If we attempt to ground our moral system on what seem to be *non*arbitrary assumptions, for example, man's universal fear of death or desire for happiness, we make the false move from saying what *is* natural to man to what *ought* to be done. In Hume's view, moral judgments are ultimately dependent on statements of emotional preferences, and are psychologically determined, mere consequences of our differing psychological makeups:

> Morality consists . . . not in any *matter of fact* . . . morality is not an object of reason. Take any action allow'd to be vicious: Wilful murder, for instance. Examine it in all lights, and see if you can find that matter of fact, or real existence, which you call *vice*. In whichever way you take it, you find only certain passions, motives, volitions, and thoughts. There is no other matter of fact in the case. The vice entirely escapes you, as long as you consider the object. You never can find it, till you turn your reflexion into your own breast, and find a sentiment of disapprobation, which arises in you, towards this action. Here is a matter of fact; but 'tis the object of feeling, not of reason. It lies in yourself, not in the object. So that when you pronounce any action or character to be vicious, you mean nothing, but that from the constitution of your nature you have a feeling or sentiment of blame from the contemplation of it. . . .[12]

Where a passion is neither founded on false suppositions, nor choses means insufficient for the end, the under-

---

[11] "A Treatise of Human Nature," in *Hume's Ethical Writings*, ed. Alisdair MacIntyre (New York and London: Collier Books, The Macmillan Co., 1965) p. 196.
[12] Ibid., p. 195.

standing can neither justify nor condemn it. 'Tis not contrary
to reason to prefer the destruction of the whole world to the
scratching of my finger.[13]

Of course it *may* be contrary to reason to have such a preference, but in Hume's view this could only be so if one contra-
dicted one's own basic assumptions. Hume's point might hold,
for example, of the extreme egoist, who starts from the basic
assumption that his own pain is the sole evil. All such choices
of basic assumptions are arbitrary, in Hume's view, and cannot
be held to be contrary to reason.

Hume's arguments remain the main stumbling blocks to
the development of a rational basis for moral judgments.
R. M. Hare's attempt in *The Language of Morals* to give an
account of our justifying moral decisions by showing that they
are in line with a "way of life to which we are committed" has
been strongly criticized. Opposed "ways of life" may be equally
well-founded and opposed decisions in particular cases may be
equally well "justified." Therefore Atkinson's meeting with the
moral philosopher leads him to conclude that irreducible
differences are possible in morality and he advises those who
are concerned with moral education to take note of this, for it
seems to him to be often assumed that there is no room for
serious dispute about what is to be taught in moral education.
In fact Atkinson refers to the prevailing climate in matters of
moral education as a "conspiracy of silence."

If Atkinson were right in his scepticism, it would be
impossible to morally educate children. It would only be possible to teach them to behave in ways which society approves,
and since the approval of society is by no means a criterion of
truth, all moral education would be a form of indoctrination if
the rules are passed on to children as if they were true. But this
position is one which ignores recent attempts to get around the
difficulty with which Hume's arguments confront us. Before we
accept Atkinson's council of despair we ought to examine
Philippa Foot's recent critique of Hare and Benn and Peters'
attempt to relate morality to rationality.

[13] Ibid., p. 180.

Foot conveniently summarizes the dilemma we have been describing as follows:

> Those who are influenced by the emotivist theory of ethics, [see the previous quotations from Hume, pp. 121–23] and yet wish to defend what Hare has called "the rationality of moral discourse," generally talk a lot about "giving reasons" for saying that one thing is right, and another wrong. The fact that moral judgements need defence seems to distinguish the impact of one man's moral views upon others from mere persuasion or coercion, and the judgements themselves from mere expressions of likes and dislikes. Yet the version of argument in morals currently accepted seems to say that, while reasons must be given, no one need accept them unless he happens to hold particular moral views. It follows that disputes about what is right and wrong can be resolved only if certain contingent conditions are fulfilled; if they are not fulfilled, the argument breaks down, and the disputants are left face to face in an opposition which is merely an expression of attitude and will. Much energy is expended in showing that no sceptical conclusion can be drawn. It is suggested, for instance, that anyone who has considered all the facts which could bear on his moral position has *ipso facto* produced a "well founded" moral judgement; in spite of the fact that anyone else who has considered the same facts may well come to the opposite conclusion. How "*x* is good" can be a well founded moral judgement when "*x* is bad" can be equally well founded it is not easy to see.[14]

Foot characterizes Hare's position as one which is governed by the thought that there is no logical connection between statements of fact and statements of value. Each man, therefore, makes his own decision as to which facts about a situation are relevant to its evaluation. Similarly no one could be reproached for failing to give reasons for statements of moral principle, since any moral argument must contain some undefended premises of this kind. Nor could he be accused of failing to meet arguments put forward by opponents arguing

[14] Philippa Foot, "Moral Arguments," *Mind*, Vol. LXVII, October, 1958, p. 502.

from different principles—all he needs to do, after all, is to deny their ultimate major premises. In Foot's view, we need to show that some things do, and some things do not, count in favor of a moral conclusion, and that a man can no more decide for himself what is evidence for rightness or wrongness than he can decide for himself what is evidence for monetary inflation or a tumor on the brain.

Before we examine Foot's attempt to show this, we must point out that Hare's position is not so simple as has been suggested. Hare's main debt is to Kant, and Hare is presenting us with a version of one of Kant's major contributions to moral theory, the principle which Kant called the "categorical imperative." The first formulation of this principle is:

Act only on that maxim which you can at the same time will to be a universal law.

Kant held that this principle, which is often called the principle of impartiality, is the means of testing whether a rule is a true rule of morality. For example, if on a particular occasion we hold that it is wrong for someone to steal, the way of testing whether this is a valid moral rule is to ask ourselves if it would be wrong for *anyone* to steal on such an occasion. The principle is the elementary one used in the moral education of children when we ask them such questions as, "How would it be if someone stole from you?" or "How would it be if everyone stole from each other?" We will return to this point when we consider Benn and Peters' moral theory. The point we are noting at present is that Hare does not say that selecting moral principles is a completely arbitrary or relative matter. He maintains that an agent must be prepared to "universalize" the principles upon which he acts if they are to be moral rules.

The major difficulty with the principle of impartiality is that it is logically possible for a man to want to universalize a principle which is quite trivial or obviously immoral (that is if *anything* is to count as immoral). What if a man holds that torturing is morally permissible and is prepared to "universalize" the practice—he is prepared to be tortured himself? What would we say to this? Foot wants to know

> How is [the torturer] supposed to have answered the objection that to inflict torture is to do harm? If he is supposed to have said that pain is good for a man in the long run, rather than bad, he will have to show the benefits involved, and he can no more choose what shall count as a benefit than he could have chosen what counted as harm.[15]

Foot is appealing to the criteria which we employ for using the concepts "harm" and "benefit." She is arguing that since you cannot use terms in any way you like if what you say is to be meaningful, you cannot justify inflicting pain on people just by calling it a "benefit." You have to produce evidence to show that it is a benefit. And in such cases, of course, this is very difficult to do.

Foot's most damning argument against the Kantian position is that completely pointless rules could be recognized as moral rules if the principle of "universalizability" is accepted as the means of deciding what are true rules of morality. Kantians are very concerned to avoid legislating against alien moral codes. They want to leave it open for us to refer to such practices as, for example, the Hindu custom of burning wives with their husband's body as exemplifying a *moral* rule. Presumably the wives are prepared to universalize the rule and to urge it on others. But they would hardly think it pointless to do this, and the Kantian ignores the *reasons* for the rule—all that is necessary is that the individual is prepared to universalize it—for *whatever* reasons. As Foot points out, the consequences are very hard to stomach. If people happened to insist that no one should run around trees left-handed, or look at hedgehogs in the light of the moon, this might count as a basic moral principle about which nothing more need be said.

Now Foot is not denying that impartiality (i.e., the readiness to universalize principles) is an essential test of a moral rule. She is arguing that it is not a *sufficient* test. Not only must we be impartial, but we must also consider the interests of people concerned—the harm or benefit which the adoption of a principle might have on others. She says,

[15] Ibid., p. 511.

I do not know what could be meant by saying that it was someone's [moral] duty to do something unless there was an attempt to show why it *mattered* if this sort of thing were not done. How can questions such as, "What does it matter?" "What harm does it do?" "What advantage is there?" "Why is it important?" be set aside here?[16]

So Foot is turning the tables on the Humean sceptic who asks, "How *can* we derive our evaluations from statements of fact?" by asking, "Where *else* can we derive them from?" To deny that the question of how a rule affects people, the harm or benefit that its adoption brings, is tantamount to refusing to accept anything as counting in favor of a moral proposition. And if the Kantian replies, "But I *do* count something—I count a man's preparedness to *universalize* his principles, his willingness to accept that everyone should adopt the principles in question," then we may ask him how he decides that a principle should be universally adopted without considering the harm and benefits that would result.

Foot's arguments lead directly into the position adopted by S. I. Benn and R. S. Peters[17] which is a combination of Kant's concern for impartiality and respect for persons with a Utilitarian concern for the consequences which the adoption of a moral rule would in fact have. Benn and Peters ask, as does Foot, "How can we exclude consideration of the interests of persons effected?" when we try to answer the Kantian question, "How would it be if everyone acted on this principle?" The great danger with the Utilitarian position in ethics is not that by looking to the consequences of the adoption of a moral rule Utilitarians are guilty of deriving "ought" from "is." (For how else can we support moral evaluations than by referring to the harm or benefit which the adoption of a rule might have?) Rather, it is that Utilitarians may ignore the importance of the principle of impartiality or respect for persons. In its crudest form, the Utilitarian test for the rightness of a moral rule is the production of the greatest happiness for the greatest number.

---

16 Ibid., p. 510.
17 *Social Principles and the Democratic State* (London: Allen and Unwin Ltd., 1965).

Used as a sole principle, this may lead to gross injustice to individuals. It then becomes possible to argue that one man ought to die for the good of the people, even if he is guiltless. Bentham's recognition of this danger led him to introduce as a corollary to the "greatest happiness" principle the additional principle, "Each is to count for one and none for more than one." This is, of course, a version of Kant's principle of impartiality and respect for persons.

Benn and Peters' most significant contribution to the attempt to establish that there are valid criteria for making moral judgments is to show the necessary connection between the principle of impartiality and being rational. They point out that "the very idea of searching for truth takes for granted a norm of *impartiality* which holds that issues should be decided according to the *relevant* criteria and that exceptions should not be made on irrelevant grounds."

> Of course, the difficulty often is to decide, in particular contexts, what *are* relevant grounds. But in this context, when the question at issue is the truth of an assertion, it is manifestly irrelevant to decide it by reference to the personal or social characteristics of the person who put forward the assertion. In the context of the search for truth impartiality amounts to being prepared to admit one's own fallibility and being prepared to admit that the other person may be right although one may dislike him personally or object to his religion, colour, social class, voice, or any other such irrelevant attributes. This criterion can be put more strongly in terms of *respect for persons*. For if we are prepared to attend seriously to what another person has to say, whatever his personal or social attributes, we must have at least a minimal respect for him as the source of an argument.[18]

Since moral discourse is rational discourse, anyone who engages seriously in the pursuit of moral truth must be committed to procedures and assumptions such as impartiality and respect for persons which are very general moral principles. It follows from this, for example, that a proposal to interfere with someone's liberty must be supported by reasons which estab-

[18] Ibid., p. 32.

lish the need for the constraint. The reasonable thing to do is to leave people alone unless you have grounds for interfering with them.

Keith Dixon has recently argued that Benn and Peters' establishment of these very general principles is of only marginal importance to the problems of moral education.

> No doubt we should teach children to be reasonable, kind and tolerant. Possibly we may have "ultimate" grounds for maintaining this. But such matters are marginal to the problems of moral education—for it is what is to count as tolerance, reasonableness and kindness in complex moral and social situations, that argument centres around.[19]

If, however, we combine Benn and Peters' justification for the moral procedural principles of impartiality and respect for persons with Foot's account of the necessity to consider the harm or benefit which the adoption of a principle might have, we can surely do *some* useful work which could appropriately be called moral education. And this has been the main point of our argument. Atkinson is right to maintain that moral education is only possible if there are criteria of truth, cogency and correctness in the field. Without such criteria we could only "indoctrinate" or "instruct" in moral matters. We have directed attention to some recent attempts to adduce such criteria in the face of Atkinson's scepticism when he calls the attention of educationalists to a view that is widely held by modern moral philosophers—"Take any moral position and its opposite can be maintained without logical error or factual mistake." We think we have offered good reasons for denying that this view can be held. Having thus established that it makes sense to speak *of* moral education, we will try to offer some sense *about* it.

(C) MORAL EDUCATION

There are a number of reasons for doubting whether teachers should play the role of moral educators at all. First, there is the

[19] "On Teaching Moral Procedures," *British Journal of Educational Studies,* Vol. XVI, No. 1, February 1968.

matter of qualifications. There seem to be good grounds for saying that a teacher of science must know a lot about science and a teacher of history a lot about history. They must have proven their knowledge and skill in science or history, usually by demonstrating their ability in these disciplines in public tests. There is, of course, no guarantee that success in such tests and the obtaining of a degree will enable them to become good teachers. But while such qualifications are not *sufficient* conditions for becoming a good teacher, they are fairly *necessary* conditions, for the qualifications usually serve as minimal guarantees that a teacher knows what history or science is about.

Yet there seem to be no remotely comparable means of determining whether a man is likely to have such minimal capacities as a moral educator. Admittedly it is unlikely that a well-known wife-beater or child-thrasher will get a teaching job. But even such active immorality needs to have earned some space in the Sunday papers if it is to disqualify anyone. Most of us have our kinky spots and most of us reading this are or will be teachers. Should most of us be moral educators, though? There is certainly no explicit attempt to discriminate among teachers in colleges of education on the basis of their ability to make moral discriminations. Ought we to rebel or cheer if this were attempted?

One of the factors which militates against the view that teachers ought to be moral educators is that they are in a position of authority with regard to children. An examination of why this should interfere with the job of moral education will involve taking the first step towards saying what moral education *means*.

In our view, if a man abstains from doing anything wrong simply because he has been told or instructed not to by some authority, his behavior can only be called *moral* behavior in a very extended sense. Certainly we do often speak of the man who does the right things and does not do the wrong things (according to some code) as morally good. But if all he is doing is following without consideration rules laid down by some authority, just because it is an authority, whether it be convention, the law or the Koran, then he is morally good only in a very weak sense. In fact it is probably inappropriate to call such behavior morally good. For could we not then refer to a dog's behavior as being morally good? If a dog follows the rules laid down by its master—doesn't bark in company, chase cars, soil carpets or fight other dogs—surely its behavior is comparable with that of a man who follows rules unquestioningly. And just as it is nonsense to speak of the *moral* goodness of a dog, so it seems to be nonsense to speak of the *moral* goodness of a man who behaves in the relevant respects like a dog.

Now a teacher does not, of course, usually behave towards children as a man does towards his dog. But in so far as he is in a position of authority in relation to children then there is some resemblance. And it will be argued in the next chapter that the teacher must, inevitably, on many occasions, resort to authority, to the rule of law. This is not because we have some sort of die-hard nostalgia for the days when chilren were seen but not heard. It is rather that we think that many of the rules that a teacher insists that children follow are extremely difficult to justify. We do not mean the petty rules, like asking permission to leave the room, or not swearing or refraining from kissing girls in the corridor. These are not *moral* rules, but quite arbitrary sanctions. In our view it should never be pretended to children that these are moral rules—far better to admit that they are quite arbitrary and irrational conventions—like standing when a woman enters the room or refraining from wearing a bathing costume in an overheated library. It is not that petty rules such as these are difficult to justify and so require the exercise of authority. They may require the exercise of authority, but they are not difficult to justify. They are simply not *capable* of any satisfactory justification. On the contrary, the rules which we have in mind as being *difficult* to justify in school situations are *moral* rules, like truth-telling, or not stealing, or not injuring one another. And if you think that these are easy to justify, consider a few typical cases:

(a) Johnny, who is poor and is the son of a criminal steals five cents from Bill who is rich and is the son of a financier.

Teacher admonishes Johnny as gently but as firmly as possible, telling him that it is wrong to steal. Johnny asks why—Bill certainly won't miss the five cents and Johnny *needed* it. How does the teacher justify the principle? He might ask Johnny how it would be if everyone stole from everyone else. To which Johnny might reply that everyone doesn't need five cents as much as he did. And so the argument might go on, until the teacher, at some point, is presumably forced to resort to warning Johnny of the consequences of stealing. This may be a very useful lesson for Johnny—he may learn that he must avoid getting caught. But it would hardly be a moral lesson.

(b) Johnny gives Bill a black eye in the playground. Teacher tries to justify the principle of non-injury, to be met with protests of, "He started it." Johnny is relying on self-defence—quite a good argument. But the teacher can never find out whether Bill *did* in fact start it, so he is forced to punish Johnny and/or Bill on the grounds that he has a responsibility to see that the children in his charge don't get injured. Johnny and /or Bill feel a sense of injustice and sense that the rules are laid down by authority and you beat them if you can get away with it. The moral rules get confused with the arbitrary conventions.

Now it could be argued that since the teacher is often forced into the position of an authority with regard to arbitrary *and* moral rules, that he is in consequence in a peculiarly bad position to play the role of moral educator, if what we primarily mean by this is someone who teaches children that there are reasons for moral rules. The time-honored argument, which crops up regularly in letters to the papers and in staff-rooms, that it's a tough world, and you have to learn to toe the line in school in order to get used to toeing it outside school, has nothing whatever to do with moral education. Toeing the line is not moral behavior any more than a dog's rule-following is moral behavior.

Nevertheless it is probably true that moral education, in the sense of developing autonomous and impartial rule-following, is not psychologically *possible* until a certain stage in a child's mental development. And it may be extremely *difficult* when the influence of the peer group is strong. Since the authority of the group will take over as soon as that of the teacher is relaxed, it may be better to have children following the *teacher's* authority-based rules, even if this militates against moral education. The requirements of safety hardly need justification, and some social conventions such as truth-telling and keeping contracts are, as Peters points out, almost part of the *definition* of a *society*—an argument which is hardly likely to count for much to a child, but one which is powerful enough to make many adults think twice about letting children's acceptance of such rules depend on their seeing and accepting the reasons for them. There are some strong arguments for saying that it is more important that a child follow certain rules than that he be morally educated. The unfortunate aspect of the proposed role of the teacher as moral educator is that it then becomes so easy for him to confuse the two—to think that merely getting children to follow rules is to morally educate them. And of course the children are even more likely to confuse authority-governed rule-following with moral behavior.

To sum up the arguments so far. Two main objections have been raised against the view that teachers should play the role of moral educators:

(a) There is no guarantee that teachers themselves are competent in moral matters.

(b) Teachers often have an authoritarian role, either because circumstances do not permit much reason giving in relation to conduct, or because the children are not mature enough to see the point of giving reasons, or because it is practically essential to transmit some rules to children whether the reasons are apparent to them or not. This authoritarian role conflicts in various ways with the role of moral educator.

So far only the devil's advocate has been heard. And although these arguments present important difficulties, it is our contention that teachers do have a role as moral educators. In fact almost any activity which can genuinely be called "educational" will have its morally educative aspects. This is a very fundamental sense of "moral education," of course. It has nothing to do with "instruction" in the fairly limited sense that people have in mind when they tell us that parents have opted out of morally educating their children and that teachers have to step in to fill the gap. The evidence for this view is obscure; even if it were true, it is far from obvious that the job ought to be passed on to teachers. Nor are we at all persuaded by the argument that society expects teachers to produce good citizens—that since teachers are employed by the State they have a duty to meet socially approved ends. In our view the teacher's obligation in this direction operates only in a negative fashion—he is probably obliged to refrain from inciting children to break the law or to be anti-social. And even if it could be argued that teachers are obliged to develop a *positive* respect for law, we have seen that this is a very weak sense of moral education. A capacity to conform is not to be confused with, and may often be opposed to, moral competence.

In what way does any educational activity have morally educative aspects? It was argued in an earlier chapter that there is a necessary connection between education and the introduction of children (or adults) into certain forms of knowledge. The study of any form of knowledge involves the use of reason, which is basic to moral education. In a penetrating section of his *Authority, Responsibility and Education*, R. S. Peters describes how "reasonableness is essential to morality" and how the requirements of impartiality and respect for other people as sources of argument are presuppositions of any reasonable discourse (pp. 32–34). What Peters is getting at in this crucial passage (which is too long to cite here) is that the *manner* of making moral judgments is closely related to, and is just as important as, the manner of making scientific or historical judgments. This manner is rational, which means that it is impartial and that it involves respect for other people as sources of argument, as points of view. By initiating children into this rational manner of making decisions we accomplish a very important part of moral education. For, as Kant points out, the main way to test whether a rule is a *moral* rule, rather than an arbitrary or biased sanction, is to ask whether it should be followed by anyone else in that situation. This is the criterion of impartiality. To introduce children to rational procedures is also to introduce them, in a very general way, to a moral way of thinking. In this sense we cannot avoid the role of moral educators. For insofar as in teaching our particular subject we develop in children a respect for others as sources of argument, a recognition of the need for giving reasons for making differences, and a questioning of arbitrary authority, then we are performing a vital role in moral education.

There is another rather different way in which our role as subject teachers merges with the role of moral educators. So far our discussion has stressed the importance of rational procedures in moral education. We have argued that the manner of making judgments in any form of rational discourse is morally educative. But we must not ignore the importance of the content of various forms of knowledge in relation to moral education. In our view it is essential to know a lot of facts, to be well informed on a wide variety of matters in order to be in a position to make effective moral judgments. Moral decisions draw on knowledge of many kinds—historical, scientific, psychological and sociological knowledge, for example, may all be useful and are sometimes essential if we are to make the right moral judgments. Thus, even everyday personal decisions may require some rudimentary psychological or sociological knowledge—some knowledge of the way people work as individuals and as groups. And, of course, the less rudimentary the knowledge is the better. Consider, for example, the principle of noninjury. This does not mean simply that we should refrain from bashing one another; it means that we should try to avoid *hurting* one another in all kinds of subtle ways. This requires sensitivity, which is not just feeling but a feeling informed by knowledge of other people. Both psychology and literature may be important here, providing an insight, scientific or intuitive, into human motivations, feelings and so on. History is a vast mine of experience which may be brought to bear on our larger, less personal moral judgments such as the rightness or wrongness of increasing M.P.'s salaries rather than pensions, or the rightness or wrongness of bombing North Vietnam. There would also seem to be a number of important moral lessons implicit in the facts of the two world wars. Perhaps a philosopher would be suspicious of the sort of connection we suggest between matters of fact and moral imperatives. But we have maintained that such concepts as "harm" or "benefit" are meaningful only in relation to what is *in fact* harmful or beneficial—and we may be better able to gauge what is harmful or beneficial, and thus what we ought to do, in the light of psychology, literature, history, etc.

We began by considering those factors which make it difficult for a teacher to be a moral educator and followed by arguing that a subject teacher, nevertheless, cannot avoid being a moral educator since there are morally educative aspects of both the procedure and the content of the subjects taught in schools. The immediately preceding arguments should have prepared the ground for the next point, which is that there is no specific *content* to moral knowledge itself. There is no organized body of moral facts or laws, and it is this which makes "moral instruction" seem a highly suspect affair. Certainly we can claim to know what is right, what is good, what ought to be done in many particular situations. There are quite distinctive reasons for claiming to know the answer to a moral problem; for example, we might say, "I know it was the right thing to do, because I would hold that anyone in my position under those circumstances would have been obliged to do it." But these are always claims to know something which refer to particular circumstances or to being in a particular position. Our knowledge is not built up as it is in science or history, although it may always be relevant to different circumstances and situations. The situations in which we find ourselves as moral agents are nearly always different and new. Moral discourse is practical discourse, it is a focus of other forms of knowledge; our knowledge of men, nature and things derived from the different disciplines is re-sorted and related to help us answer the moral or practical question. "What ought I to do?" "What is the right thing to do?" So that if schools were to make a special place in the curriculum for moral education it would have to be a meeting place of various disciplines. It would be held together by concentrating on moral (or "practical") problems and would draw on knowledge from a wide variety of fields in the effort to solve the problems. It is because moral education does imply a wide coverage of other fields of knowledge that we speak of it as we do as moral *education*. For we do not speak of "history education" or "science education," but rather of *training* someone in history or science. Whereas *moral* training implies rigid behavior according to a code of rules. By moral *education* we mean that there will be a wide cognitive perspective—that knowledge derived from specialist forms of thought will be tapped and seen to be relevant to practical and personal dilemmas.

But is this enough? Are we satisfied that a child is morally educated if he becomes skilled at *seeing* how he ought to act? Do we not usually insist that moral education has only been effective if it is reflected in children's behavior? Usually we insist that not only must children come to know *what* is right and to know *how* to work out what is right, but they must also act in a way which shows that their knowledge influences their conduct. Whereas we can surely claim to have successfully taught history or science without looking at a child's conduct. This presents us with a difficult problem which will be tackled in the next section.

(D) THE CHARACTER ASPECT OF MORAL EDUCATION

As we are all aware, we may *know* what is right, what we *ought* to do, and still do what is wrong. Socrates denied that this was so—he held that we always do what we think right. If Socrates was correct, the job of moral education would be made much easier. For although the knowledge aspect of moral education is, as was argued in the previous section, a delicate and subtle matter, the *character* aspect of moral education is even more elusive. It would be extremely convenient not to have to concern ourselves with how children behaved— to be able to sit back after a few years with a group and say, "Well, I've done all I can to make those children into autonomous and impartial moral agents, and so far as I can test it, they not only know a lot about moral questions, they know how to work out for themselves what is right, i.e., they can draw on their knowledge intelligently." But what if you invite the group to your home one evening and a number of valuables is missing the following morning? It is almost inconceivable that the thief was doing what he thought right. And we would certainly have good reason for doubting that we'd morally educated the thief. For although he knew what was right, his knowledge did not affect his conduct. Except in cases of mental disorder, we refer to such a gap between knowing what is right and doing what is right as due to weakness of will or weakness of character. The weak-willed person, or the person of weak character is easil tempted, easily corrupted or led astray. And if we think that moral education should be reflected in conduct then we must give some consideration to what is involved in character education (or as it is usually expressed the "training of character").

There are two main ways of thinking about character; there is the noncommittal sense, when we speak of a man's character as the sum total of his traits, whether they are good *or* bad traits. The noncommittal sense is exemplified when we simply describe objectively what a man's characteristics are in a kind of report—we may say, for example, that he is dishonest, determined, punctual, careful and mean. But this neutral, descriptive sense of "character" must be distinguished from "having character," which is what we mean when we refer to a man "of character." These are terms of praise and they refer to the kind of thing we want to develop in character education. Peters sets it out most lucidly. He says that when we speak of character in this way, we don't mean to refer to any particular traits,

> . . . but the claim is made that whatever traits are ex-
> hibited there will be some sort of control or consistency in
> the manner in which he exhibits them. He will not give way
> to his inclinations, be easily corrupted, or take his colour
> from his company. . . . A man who "has character" may
> present an appearance of inconsistency to the world . . .

but his variations in rule-following cannot be correlated with the strength of his inclinations or with the persistence of social pressures. He follows rules which seem to him to have some point and modifies them intelligently according to differences in circumstances; and the point, to a large extent is determined by his adherence to certain higher order principles. . . . These principles may be limited in scope, like those of Colonel Nicholson in "The Bridge on the River Kwai," whose principles were that an officer should care for his men, obey a superior officer, and honour international conventions. Or they might be more general ones, such as one ought not to exploit others to further one's own interest or that one ought to minimize avoidable misery. Or they might be morally suspect principles, such as that one ought always to further the interests of one's country, church or party. A man would have character to the extent to which he was impervious to temptation or to social pressures in applying rules intelligently in the light of such supreme principles. But of course he might have character—and be bad.[20]

That last remark is extremely important. For if a man may have character and be bad it is obvious that character education is only a part of moral education. It presupposes that children have been brought to know what is in general right and wrong and to know how to decide for themselves in difficult cases (this knowledge aspect was the concern of the previous section). Just as moral education seems incomplete if children do not come to act in accordance with what they know to be right, so it seems incomplete if they consistently act in accordance with principles—but principles which are wrong or limited in scope. It is essential to grasp these two ways in which moral education may be lopsided. The first is straightforward enough—the children may know what rules are and be able to modify principles in relation to moral problems in a rational, autonomous way, but they still *do* what they know to be wrong. This is a result of neglecting character training (except in cases of mental disorder). But it would be quite

[20] *Authority, Responsibility and Education,* pp. 113–15.

possible to educate children "of character"—children who "have character," who are nevertheless bad. For although they may act in accordance with principles and modify them intelligently when faced with moral dilemmas, they may be following and choosing amongst bad principles. They would be autonomous, but just not know enough about right and wrong.

But perhaps this point is being labored and perhaps the question that is looming large is "How does one go about developing character?" You may well think that understanding what is meant by moral education is important and may even agree that character education is part of it, but how does one go about educating children to follow principles in a way that showed that the children "have character?"

There is much that is mysterious about this question. We can however be fairly sure that the manner of carrying out the knowledge aspect of moral education is decisive for developing the feeling for principles in children—a feeling without which they may be easily corrupted or tempted to do what they know to be wrong. But just what *is* the appropriate manner may be extremely variable, depending a lot on the particular children and on their intelligence, background and so on. Whatever is the appropriate manner on a particular occasion, it is probably by means of procedure and presentation that the moral educator will get children to think of doing right as attractive.

But doing right does not have to be made attractive. It must, surely, be thought to be attractive in itself. Surely doing what is right is not a grind, any more than doing history or science is a grind. If we are a teacher of science or of history then presumably we care for these subjects, we have a feeling for them,—not because of anything they lead to outside themselves, but for the intrinsic satisfactions they offer. We do not have to make these subjects attractive by offering prizes or rewards. The rewards are to be found in the activities themselves—they are endlessly fascinating and stimulating. If we don't find our subject to be intrinsically attractive, if we don't feel that it is worth doing for its own sake, then we ought not to teach it. To put it even more strongly, it is doubtful if we could be said to *be* educated, let alone in a position to educate others, if we have not come to *care* about the activities in which we are engaged. Such persons might be well trained but not educated.

Part of the reason why people come to feel that doing history or science is valuable and interesting is that they have been introduced to these activities by others who have experienced the kind of satisfaction these subjects offer. And why should this not be equally the case with regard to moral education? The difficulties presented by the problem of character education no longer seem insuperable if we can expect that the teacher who is morally educating really cares about doing what is right and not doing what is wrong. The difficulties in moral education will be insuperable, of course, if what the teacher understands by "right" and "wrong" is dictated by narrow sectarian prejudices which equate morality with various forms of abstinence. But if the teacher knows the satisfaction to be derived from following principles, from following "duty" rather than "desire," as Kant put it, he will transmit the sense of the intrinsic attraction of moral behavior to his pupils by all kinds of subtle means—his tone of voice, attitude to their questions, attention to their difficulties will all convey his feeling for his subject. There can be little possibility of imitating it. This does not mean, of course, that the good teacher is the one who bubbles. It is difficult to precisely identify or characterize a teacher's feeling for his subject. It varies in its manifestations from one person to another, but the effect is contagious, for children are extremely sensitive to the "feeling-tone" of a teacher. This sensitivity is most obviously apparent in the pupil's personal relationships with his teacher, but pupils are often equally sensitive to the feeling that a teacher has for his subject. They resist the bubbling enthusiast as frequently as they dislike the cynic or are bored with mere efficiency. But they will pick up a genuine interest in a subject from teachers who have widely different personalities.

Our conclusion, then, is that the problem of character education is part of a difficulty in any kind of education. Unless the *teacher* is educated, so that he has come to care for his subject and to think it worth doing for its own sake, there can be little hope that his charges will become educated—though they might be admirably trained. Similarly, if the moral educator genuinely feels that following the right rules is satisfying and rewarding then his example should go a long way towards transmitting, by a kind of contagion, such a feeling in his pupils. And since a man of character is a man who is not easily corrupted, or led to *do* what he knows to be wrong, he is likely to be a man who finds it *satisfying* to do what he knows (i.e., judges) to be right. When we consider the corrupting influences to which we are exposed—the endless bad films, bad television, bad journalism which imply that the kicks come from doing what we know to be wrong and that doing what we know to be right is a grind, the emphasis must be put on the positive and elusive satisfaction to be derived from doing what we know to be right.

SECTION (A)

Basic References

BENN, S. I. AND PETERS, R. S., *Social Principles and the Democratic State,* chapter 7. London: Allen and Unwin, Ltd., 1959.

PEARS, D. F. ed., *Freedom and the Will,* London: Macmillan and Co., Ltd., 1965.

PETERS, R. S., *Authority, Responsibility and Education,* Part II. London: Allen and Unwin, Ltd., 1959.

Further References

AYER, A. J., "Freedom and Necessity," *Philosophical Essays.*

FOOT, P., "Freewill as Involving Determinism," *Philosophical Review,* Vol. LXVI, October, 1957.

Discussion/Essay Topics

* John Hospers offers the following account of the genesis of a "normal" decision:

Leaving aside the question of how clearly and on what grounds one can distinguish the neurotic from the normal, let me use an illustration of a proclivity that everyone would call normal, namely, the decision of a man to support his wife and possibly a family, and consider briefly its genesis, according to psychoanalytic accounts.

Every baby comes into the world with a full-fledged case of megalomania—interested only in himself, acting as if believing that he is the center of the universe and that others are present only to fulfill his wishes, and furious when his own wants are not satisfied immediately no matter for what reason. Gratitude, even for all the time and worry and care expended on him by the mother, is an emotion entirely foreign to the infant, and as he grows older it is inculcated in him only with the greatest difficulty; his natural tendency is to assume that everything that happens to him is due to himself, except for denials and frustrations, which are due to the "cruel, denying" outer world, in particular the mother; and that he owes nothing to anyone, is dependent on no one. This omnipotence-complex, or illusion of non-dependence, has been called the "autarchic fiction". Such a conception of the world is actually fostered in the child by the conduct of adults, who automatically attempt to fulfill the infant's every wish concerning nourishment, sleep, and attention. The child misconceives causality and sees in these wish-fulfillments not the results of maternal kindness and love, but simply the result of his own omnipotence.

This fiction of omnipotence is gradually destroyed by experience, and its destruction is probably the deepest disappointment of the early years of life. First if all, the infant discovers that he is the victim of organic urges and necessities: hunger, defecation, urination. More important, he discovers that the maternal breast, which he has not previously distinguished from his own body (he has not needed to, since it was available when he wanted it), is not a part of himself after all, but of another creature upon whom he is dependent. He is forced to recognize this, e.g., when he wants nourishment and it is at the moment not present; even a small delay is most damaging to the "autarchic fiction". Most painful of all is the experience of weaning, probably the greatest tragedy in every baby's life, when his dependence is most cruelly emphasized; it is a frustrating experience because what he wants is no longer there at all; and if he has been able to some extent to preserve the illusion of non-dependence heretofore, he is not able to do so now—it is plain that the source of his nourishment is not dependent on him, but he on it. The shattering of the autarchic fiction is a great disillusionment to every child, a tremendous blow to his ego which he will, in one way or another, spend the rest of his life trying to repair. How does he do this?

First of all, his reaction to frustration is anger and fury; and he responds by kicking, biting, etc., the only ways he knows. But he is motorically helpless, and these measures are ineffective, and only serve to emphasize his dependence the more. Moreover, against such responses of the child the parental reaction is one of prohibition, often involving deprivation of attention and affection. Generally the child soon learns that this form of rebellion is profitless, and brings him more harm than good. He wants to respond to frustration with violent aggression, and at the same time learns that he will be punished for such aggression, and that in any case the latter is ineffectual. What face-saving solution does he find? Since he must "face facts", since he must in any case "conform" if he is to have any peace at all, he tries to make it seem as if he himself is the source of the commands and prohibitions: the *external* prohibitive force is *internalized*—and here we have the origin of conscience. By making the prohibitive agency seem to come from within himself, the child can "save face"—as if saying, "The prohibition comes from within me, not from outside, so I'm not subservient to external rule, I'm only obeying rules I've set up myself," thus to some extent saving the autarchic fiction, and at the same time avoiding unpleasant consequences directed against himself by complying with parental commands.

Moreover, the boy has unconsciously never forgiven the mother for his dependence on her in early life, for nourishment and all other things. It has upset his illusion of non-dependence. These feelings have been repressed and are not remembered; but they are acted out in later life in many ways—e.g., in the constant deprecation man has for woman's duties such as cooking and housework of all sorts ("All she does is stay at home and get together a few meals, and she calls that work"), and especially in the man's identification with the mother in his sex experiences with women. By identifying with someone one cancels out in effect the person with whom he identifies—replacing that person, unconsciously denying his existence, and the man, identifying with his early mother, playing the active role in "giving" to his wife as his mother has "given" to him, is in effect the denial of his mother's existence, a fact which is narcissistically embarrassing to his ego because it is chiefly responsible for shattering his autarchic fiction. In supporting his wife, he can unconsciously deny that his mother gave to him, and that he was dependent on her giving. Why is it that the husband plays the provider, and wants his wife to be dependent on no one else, although twenty years before he was nothing but a parasitic baby? This is a face-saving device on his part: he can act out the reasoning "See, I'm not the parasitic baby, on the contrary I'm the provider, the giver." His playing the provider is a constant face-saving device, to deny his early dependence which is so embarrassing to his ego. It is no wonder that men generally dislike to be reminded of their babyhood, when they were dependent on woman.

Thus we have here a perfectly normal adult reaction which is unconsciously motivated. The man "chooses" to support a family— and his choice is as unconsciously motivated as anything could be. (I have described here only the "normal" state of affairs, uncomplicated by the well-nigh infinite number of variations that occur in actual practice.) (John Hospers, from: Readings in Ethical Theory, Selected and Edited by Wilfred Sellars and John Hospers. © 1952. Reprinted by permission of Appleton-Century-Crofts, Division of Meredith Corporation.)

Do you think criticisms of this account, which are advanced on pp. 110–114 are justified?

* In what ways is the view that men are generally responsible for their actions modified in the case of children?

* . . . to say that my actions proceed from my character, or more colloquially, that I act in character, is to say that my behaviour is consistent and to that extent predictable; and since it is, above all, for the actions that I perform in character that I am held to be morally responsible, it looks as if the admission of moral responsibility, so far from being incompatible with determinism, tends rather to presuppose it. But how can this be so if it is a necessary condition of moral responsibility that the person who is held responsible should have acted freely? It seems that if we are to retain this idea of moral responsibility, we must either show that men can be held responsible for actions which they do not do freely, or else find some way of reconciling determinism with the freedom of the will. . . . (A. J. Ayer, "Freedom and Necessity," *Philosophical Essays*, p. 276.)

Is this a genuine dilemma? If not, why not? If so, how would you go about resolving it?

SECTION (B)

Basic References

ATKINSON, R. F., "Instruction and Indoctrination," *Philosophical Analysis and Education,* ed. R. D. Archambault. London: Routledge and Kegan Paul, Ltd., 1965.

BENN, S. I. AND PETERS, R. S., *Social Principles and the Democratic State,* Chapter 2.

FOOT, P., "Moral Arguments" *Mind*, 1958.

HARE, R. M., "Decisions of Principle," *Philosophy and Education*, 2d ed., ed. I. Scheffler. Boston: Allyn and Bacon, Inc., 1966.

HUME, D., *A Treatise on Human Nature*, particularly Part I. *Hume's Ethical Writings*, ed. Alisdair MacIntyre. New York and London; Collier Books, The Macmillan Co., 1965.

PETERS, R. S., *Ethics and Education*. London: Allen and Unwin, Ltd., 1966.

Further References

FOOT, P., "Moral Beliefs," *Proceedings of the Aristotelian Society*, 1958–9.

———, "Goodness and Choice," *Proceedings of the Aristotelian Society*, supp. vol., 1961.

HARE, R. M., *The Language of Morals*, Part 2.

HOSPERS, J., *Human Conduct: An Introduction to the Problems of Ethics*. New York: Harcourt, Brace & World, Inc., 1961.

KANT, I., *Foundations of the Metaphysics of Morals*.

MILL, J. S., *Utilitarianism*.

NOWELL-SMITH, P. H., *Ethics*.

SEARLE, J. R., "How to Derive 'Ought' from 'Is'," *Philosophical Review*, 1964, vol. 73.

Essay/Discussion Topics

* Take a factual statement, such as that Hitler persecuted the Jews. If I produce all the relevant evidence, documents and witnesses, it would be absurd for somebody to ask, 'Why is all that a reason for saying that Hitler persecuted the Jews?'; but if I give my reasons for saying that Hitler was wrong to persecute the Jews, it does always make sense to ask, 'Why is that a reason?' It seems as if moral reasons can always be challenged, whereas factual ones cannot, beyond a certain point. (Bernard Mayo, *Ethics and the Moral Life*. London: Macmillan & Co., 1958.)

Discuss.

* What are the characteristic limitations and advantages of the Kantian and Utilitarian positions in ethics?

* Catholicism inhibited the development of morality by its stress on the authority of the Church hierarchy in matters of right and wrong. This raises the question of how moral rules are to be distinguished from religious ones—a very difficult question in view of their similarity of content. Probably the answer would be that a rule is specifically religious if it is thought to have been laid down by some divinely inspired individual or group of individuals or if the individual himself regards the rule as revealed to him personally by God, and if the divine nature of its origin is thought to be the justification for obeying it. A religious rule does not have the same connection with man's reason as is usually claimed for moral rules; it depends much more on the authority of a man." (Benn and Peters, *Social Principles and the Democratic State*. London: Allen & Unwin, Ltd., 1965.)

Discuss.

SECTION (C)

Basic References

ATKINSON, R. F., "Instruction and Indoctrination," *Philosophical Analysis and Education*.

HARE, R. M., "Adolescents into Adults" *Aims in Education*, ed. T. H. B. Hollins.

PETERS, R. S., *Authority, Responsibility and Education*, Chapter 9.

————, *Ethics and Education*.

————, "Reason and Habit: The Paradox of Moral Education," *Philosophy and Education*.

WILSON, JOHN, et al., *Introduction to Moral Education* (G. B. Penguin Books, 1967).

Further References

HIRST, P. H., "Morals, Religion and the Maintained School," *British Journal of Educational Studies*, No. 1965, pp. 5–18.

KOHLBERG, L., *The Development of Children's Orientations Towards a Moral Order*.

PIAGET, J., *The Moral Judgment of the Child*. New York: Free Press.

Essay/Discussion Topics

* What is the difference between instruction in morals and moral education?

* Piaget shows that children up to the age of about seven years are incapable of appreciating that rules could be otherwise and that there are reasons for them. Questions about the validity of rules make little sense for them. R. S. Peters says about this that it is "therefore pretty pointless making their acceptance of rules at an early age depend upon them seeing the reasons for them." Should we not, then, give reasons to children under seven for following rules?

* A syllabus to help school pupils understand and cope with problems affecting school work and their life after they leave school is being prepared by the N.S.W. Education Department. One of the most enthusiastic supporters of the scheme, Mr. Norman Jenkins, the principal guidance officer in the department, said yesterday; 'We want to involve the kids. Get them thinking about important problems—morals, ethics, politics, drugs—in fact anything that could cause them trouble. . . . We will have people coming to talk to them for about two lessons a week. But, of course, this sort of thing can't be taught—it's not a chalk-and-talk sort of subject'. (Report in an Australian newspaper)

Critically examine this approach to moral education.

* Is moral education independent of religious education?

SECTION (D)

Basic References

FRANKENA, W. K., "Toward a Philosophy of Moral Education," *Philosophy and Education.*

PETERS, R. S., *Authority, Responsibility and Education*, Chapter 9.

———, "Moral Education and the Psychology of Character," *Philosophy and Education.*

Further References

KOHLBERG, L., "Development of Moral Character and Moral Ideology," *Review of Child Development Research*, vol. I, ed. M. L. Hoffman and L. W. Hoffman. New York: Russell Sage, 1964.

Essay/Discussion Topics

* In Chapter 9 of *Authority, Responsibility and Education*, Peters stresses the connection between having a critical and trained mind and "having character." If we were successful in producing children who were "autonomous" in this way, might we nevertheless have failed in the task of moral education?

* In what ways (if any) do you think that the subject you teach might be contributory to moral education? May there be some danger in being concerned with moral education in teaching some subjects?

6

Social
Principles
in
Education

(A) AUTHORITY AND CONSTRAINT
IN EDUCATION

WHAT ARE THE APPROPRIATE FUNCTIONS
and limitations of authority in schools? We have observed that
teachers frequently have to insist that children follow rules
which are based on institutionalized authority and that this is
one of the ways in which school organization resembles the
administration of a society. This resemblance between social
organization and school organization has led educational
philosophers to draw heavily on arguments derived from social
philosophy in their discussions of freedom and authority in
schools. In some respects this has been fruitful. R. S. Peters has
argued convincingly, for example, that schools need to ad-
minister a system of rules to maintain conditions of order
within which worthwhile activities can take place. It is, of
course, a purely contingent matter that teachers are handed
this job. In some educational systems order is kept by people

other than teachers who are thus relieved of the "policeman's" job. But when we recall how crucial and complex in moral education is the business of getting children to follow rules, we may wonder whether it is advisable to allow this function to be performed by school "policemen." The point is that the maintenance of order in schools is significantly different from the maintenance of order in society at large; in schools we are not concerned merely to get the children to *conform* to the rules. We ultimately want them to follow rules because they can see the reasons for them. This has led some experimental educators such as A. S. Neill[1] to largely forego the "maintenance of order" at Summerhill School in order to encourage the development of autonomous rule-following in the children. Neill would not put it like this, and would emphasize the "freedom" of the children. The fact remains, however, that a "free" school (or society) is hard to conceive if what is meant is the complete absence of rules, constraints and authority. This is plainly not what is being attempted at Summerhill, where self-government is the recurrent emphasis. Furthermore the children are not merely allowed to govern—they do not decide for themselves whether to have a school parliament.

It seems obvious that there is a necessity for a background of constraint, a rule of law in schools. This view of the function of authority in schools is succinctly expressed by Peters when he says that the task of education is to get children to transform their wants and "to use constraints to develop new wants." But there is a very great danger here. It may be considered legitimate to use constraints as a means of actually trying to pass on the skills and knowledge which form the content of education. Whereas something has surely gone wrong when teachers "use constraints to develop new wants" by insisting that a child write an essay under threat of punishment or get children to learn things by telling them that they will be garbagemen if they don't pass the exams (a sort of "psychological constraint").

This is not to deny that, with schools as they are, it may be quite reasonable or expedient to act in such ways (just as it is

---

[1] See, for example, *The Free Child* (London: Herbert Jenkins, 1953).

often expedient to merely get children to conform to rules whether they see the reasons for them or not). We may still produce children who have come to care for the educational activities which we hold to be valuable; that is, these constraints may be used as tricks to get a child started on something. But the point of using such techniques must surely be to get a child started so that he comes to see the interest and value of what is being taught. There can be no place in an educational system for the teacher who cannot see the intrinsic interest and fascination of his subject—if he has not come to care for it, then he is not educated. No doubt, this is unrealistic. We are under no delusions about the extent to which the schools constitute an educational system. But granted that educated teachers will themselves be able to educate their pupils, they must necessarily be opposed to extrinsic motivations of the kind mentioned, except as a means of getting a child started on a subject so that he may at least begin to see its intrinsic interest.

We have argued that it is generally inappropriate to use constraint as motivation for learning and conceded the necessity for constraints as a means of enforcing a background of order in schools. These points are relatively straightforward. Unfortunately, however, the whole question of the nature and function of constraints in education has been befogged by the frequent and reckless use of the term "authoritarian." This term is frequently employed by "progressive" educators, for example, to describe any teaching methods of which they disapprove. The basic point which is overlooked is that there is no need at all to associate the recognition that a teacher is *in* authority over those he teaches or *an* authority on the subject he teaches with any particular method of teaching. There is no reason why teaching methods of the sort favored by "progressive" educators—project or assignment methods, group work and discovery methods—may not be employed by a teacher who is an authority and who is in authority. In fact, to deny that a teacher is to some extent an authority on what he is teaching is tantamount to saying he is incompetent. And to deny that a teacher is in authority seems to question his institutional status. There can be little doubt that those who reject the view that a teacher ought to be to some extent an authority on the subject he teaches are themselves incompetent in the subject—hence the inflation of technique at the expense of content. We might argue, however, that those who deny that a teacher needs to be to some extent an authority on his subject ought not to be in authority. The institutional status and the various powers that accompany it ought to derive from the teacher's being, to some extent, an authority in his field.

No doubt the teacher's authority can be misused. No one wants indoctrination or Gradgrind techniques in schools. But this is not to say that there is no place for what Lewin, Lippitt and White, in their famous study,[2] called "authoritarian" forms of teaching. Since much of the revulsion from the notion that teachers ought to be authorities stems from this piece of work, let us see what they describe as the four characteristics of authoritarian teaching:

1. All determination of policy by the leader.
2. Techniques and activity steps dictated by the authority, one at a time, so that future steps were always uncertain to a large degree.
3. The leader usually dictated the particular work task and work companions of each member.
4. The dominator was "personal" in his praise and criticism of the work of each member, but remained aloof from active group participation except when demonstrating. He was friendly or impersonal rather than openly hostile.[3]

Whatever was found in this experiment about the levels of aggression in a group which was controlled in this way, we might still insist that a teacher may legitimately employ such techniques on numerous occasions. Children frequently need to be *told* things. They need to be instructed. There is nothing sacrosanct about getting children to find things out for themselves. But at what cost, you may ask. What did Lewin, Lippett and White find out about the level of aggression in a

2 "Patterns of Agressive Behaviour in Experimentally Created 'Social Climates,'" *The Journal of Social Psychology*, 1939, no. 10.
3 Ibid., p. 273.

group controlled in an "authoritarian" way in relation to a "democratically" controlled group, in which "all policies were a matter of group discussion and decision," the group members were free to choose their own workmates, and the leader tried to be a "regular group member?" Incredibly enough, given the way the research has been so widely thought to have invalidated authoritarian methods, they found that over all the groups the level of aggression in authoritarian groups was *lower* than in the democratically run group.

D. W. Harding sums up what took place most effectively:

> If Lewin had been living contentedly in a totalitarian state he would almost certainly have left it at that and congratulated himself on the striking support his political convictions had received from the strictest experimental investigation. Surely scientists with a bias towards authoritarian regimes might plausibly claim that Lewin *should* have left it at that or at least left the emphasis on his numerical results, since they gave the nearest approach to impartiality and objectivity of all the records he could make.
>
> But Lewin was an exile from an authoritarian regime, living in the United States and loyal to the democracy he found there. He went beyond the numerical results of his experiment and reported very interesting qualitative observations strongly suggesting that the freedom from acts of aggression under authoritarian leadership went with a rather crushed, apathetic spirit among the boys and reflected only the restrictive influence of the leader. In the discussion of the results, the whole emphasis is placed on the relatively intangible advantages of democratic control, and not on the numerical results from which the greatest promise of scientific rigour had seemed to come.[4]

It would probably be foolish to adopt authoritarian methods for the tasks which Lewin, Lippitt and White set for the children in their experiment, for example. It is not widely known that the children in the "clubs" (not schoolrooms) were occupied entirely with craftwork, particularly

---

[4] Harding, *Social Psychology and Individual Values* (London: Hutchinson's University Library, 1953), p. 106.

making masks. If we look back to the four characteristics of the "authoritarian" control, it is hardly surprising that there was a good deal of apathy among children who were told step by step how to make a mask, for this is the sort of activity where there obviously ought to be a good deal of room for individual initiative. But it seems to be eminently sensible to tell children that the earth moves around the sun or that the peasants played an important part in the French Revolution or that you do a quadratic equation in the following manner. By all means use models, documents, pictures, etc. to illustrate and make real where possible. But there are many things which it is unreasonable to expect a child to find out for himself. And such irrationality is usually the product of a misconception of authority.

A useful distinction to bear in mind when deciding what teaching contexts are appropriate ones for the exercise of authoritarian methods is the distinction (referred to earlier, p. 65) between "closed" and "open" competences. The teaching of closed competences seems far more suited to the use of such methods than teaching open competences. This distinction (made by Professor Passmore in a lecture at the University of London in June 1967) may be exemplified as follows: we might teach someone to play chess in such a way that he is only able to make the moves he has actually been taught to make, so that his games are always routines and needn't require much attention. Or we might teach someone French so that he was capable only of making statements in French which he had actually been taught to make. This would be to teach chess and French as closed competences and we might make a machine which could carry out these tasks. Teaching closed competences may be a stage towards the acquisition of open competences, the test for which is that the pupil can take steps which he has not been taught to make—he works out moves in chess for himself or makes a statement in French which he has not been specifically taught. Leavis' account of Wordsworth's creative processes as "spontaneity supervening upon complex development" and Coleridge's assertion that the artist needs to know "the laws of grammar, logic and psychology" before the imagination can be effective refers to the same sort of distinction. The inappropriateness of such "authoritarian" methods as instruction and telling for teaching "open" competences such as writing poetry, conversing in French or making new moves in chess is obvious. But it may be necessary or expedient to teach a number of closed competences before success in the open competences can be expected. And the techniques and skills of closed competences may be most efficiently taught by "authoritarian" methods. Whereas making masks, as was observed earlier, is not likely to be well taught by merely authoritarian methods; it is, in large part, an open competence, requiring freedom and flexibility of experimentation.

The following main points have been argued in this section:

1. The exercise of authority to constrain children in schools may be justified in two connected contexts:
   (i) As a means of getting children started on activities which teachers think to be *in* their interest but in which the children are not initially interested.
   (ii) As a means of enforcing a background of order in a classroom so that a situation is created in which worthwhile activities may take place.

2. Extrinsic motivation ought to give way to intrinsic motivation as soon as it becomes practicable. If education is to take place, it is essential that the children come to care for the intrinsic interest of a subject.

3. The abnegation of authority on the part of progressive educationists is usually to be associated with a confusion between the methods and the content of teaching. Discovery methods are frequently a preferable way of teaching some subjects, but it is a foolish ideology which denies that authoritarian techniques such as instruction are often both useful and necessary.

(B) FREEDOM IN EDUCATION

The key argument of this section is that all that is meant by the term "free" is the absence of some constraint or constraints. In our view, all the efforts which have been made to suggest that to be free implies something positive are evaluations in the disguise of analysis. Aristotle thought that our conception of freedom as merely the absence of some constraint or constraints was a mean conception. This reaction is understandable, for "freedom" is a laudatory word and is frequently associated with desirable or valuable states of affairs. We are, nevertheless, prepared to sacrifice the emotional kicks of a more high-flown conception for accuracy in the analysis. The emotive connotations of "freedom" should not lead us into a mistaken view of what it means. For it makes perfectly good sense to say "I am free to cheat my friends" or "I am free to tell lies when it pleases me," although my freedom to behave in these ways is not worth going to the barricades for.

The view that freedom means, at least in part, the imposition of restraints is put forward very persuasively by Professor Bantock. He follows Cranston[5] in distinguishing between two uses of the notion of freedom—"freedom from" and "freedom to." "Freedom from" is "negative freedom" according to Bantock; it is freedom from constraint of some kind. "Freedom to" is "positive freedom" and Professor Bantock elsewhere refers to it as "true freedom" or "rational freedom."

> What I do mean is that "true" human freedom does not spring from the unrestrained indulgence of desires or impulses, though that does not mean that no desire or impulse should be allowed—it all depends on their nature. What the attainment of "true" freedom involves is some measure of restraint; it is, in fact, something to be realised, not something to be accepted.[6]

The danger here is that "some measure of restraint" seems to be considered as part of what is meant by "true freedom," whereas in our view freedom can only mean that some constraints or restraints are absent. Professor Bantock points out that nearly all philosophers have found in the absence of

[5] Maurice Cranston, *Freedom: A New Analysis* (London: Longmans, 1967).

[6] G. H. Bantock, *Education and Values* (London: Faber and Faber, 1965) p. 99.

restraint an insufficient view of what constitutes human freedom" and he argues that

> . . . doing as one wants may very well lead to interference with someone else's desire to do what he wants, which, in revenge, might lead him to interfere with what one wants to do. Hence the elementary principle that what one wants to do ought not to interfere with the freedom of others sprang up, and desire becomes tempered with morality. Hence, too, the development of the view that freedom springs, not from following the unrestraints of impulse and desire, but from allowing one's desires to be sifted by reason; another version of the same basic idea emerges from the belief that freedom springs from the observation of the moral law.[7]

Now all this may very well be true. Certainly we do limit our freedom to do what we want out of consideration for others, either because we have to or because we think this is morally right or the rational thing to do. But what must be retained is that if our freedom is limited by moral or unavoidable constraints then it is indeed limited. However necessary or desirable the limitations or constraints are, it is always incorrect to refer to the imposition of limitations or constraints as in themselves extensions of one's freedom. Certainly as Professor Bantock points out, the acceptance of constraint may open up fields of endeavor from which we have been debarred. Thus, for example, if we lock up children for six or seven hours a day in a school we may free them from their ignorance and give them freedom to engage in activities otherwise inaccessible to them, but insofar as we are constraining people then we are constraining them. There is no such paradox as the "paradox of freedom"—"true freedom" does not mean "some measure of restraint."

The "paradox of freedom" is the phrase adopted by Professor Peters, and it has been popular among other social philosophers. Benn and Peters say that "It is the paradox of freedom that we must set a restraint to catch a restraint."[8] The

[7] Ibid., p. 98.
[8] S. I. Benn and R. S. Peters, *Social Principles and the Democratic State* (London: Allen and Unwin, Ltd., 1959) p. 213.

point of this aphorism is that if there are no restraints on men, through law or custom or morality, for example, we usually have the rise of the bully or the tyrant. To teachers it is a matter of common observation that if a new teacher fails to get control of a class, i.e., is unable to impose constraints, the resulting situation is not one of freedom for the individuals in the classroom, but the rule of the leaders in horseplay. The constraints imposed by the need to conform with the peer group are often stronger than the teacher could hope to impose.

We are not, then, out of sympathy with Bantock's and Peter's views on the needs for restraints, especially in education. What we are opposing is the view that the restraints are, in a paradoxical way, extensions of our freedom. If there is a paradox here, then it is not a conceptual paradox, for there is nothing in the concept of freedom that implies any kind of constraint.[9] In fact, what freedom *means* is that there is an absence of some kind of constraint. Any kind of constraint, any kind of interference *means* an abridgement of our freedom.

Given that we agree with the fundamental evaluations and preferences of Bantock and Peters, why is such a fuss being made about this little definitional point? Our obstinacy is a result of imagining what might result if we were to ignore the point. If we once allow that freedom might imply, even paradoxically, some kind of constraint, we've performed a great service to the bureaucrat and the dictator. The "safeguards" of liberty may then be multiplied literally in the name of *freedom*. Freedom from moral and political corruption may be safeguarded by rigorous censorship on the press and on speech. If we were to object that such constraints are *limitations* of our freedom, the bureaucrat reminds us of our admission that freedom could *mean* restraining people. We are then forced on to the far more difficult ground of arguing that freedom of speech or of the press is more valuable than freedom from

---

[9] Professor Peters makes this plain in his *Ethics and Education*. He points out (p. 187) that to see constraint as part of what is meant by freedom, ". . . is to confuse what looks like a general empirical condition of 'freedom' having concrete application with the meaning of 'freedom.' "

corruption. Whereas, if we make quite clear that *any* kind of constraint is a limitation of freedom, then the onus is on those who want to introduce the constraint to prove that it is justified. But we will give away our strongest card if to begin with we agree that part of what being free means is that we are subject to some kinds of constraints.

Professor Bantock's suggestion that "true freedom" implies some kind of constraint is derived partly from his distinction between "negative freedom" and "positive freedom," or "freedom from" and "freedom to." There is nothing wrong with saying that the most valuable kind of freedom is "freedom to"—especially since Professor Bantock's essay is on freedom in education. Certainly an education which involves the initiation of children into forms of knowledge and a tradition of disciplined endeavor towards understanding may involve numerous restraints. And Professor Bantock's defence in terms of the positive value which these restraints may produce is in line with the conception of education advanced throughout this book—that education implies that something of value is going on. But the distinction between "freedom from" and "freedom to" is an artificial and not at all helpful prop to Bantock's argument. As Cranston points out,[10] the distinction leads nowhere; all cases of "freedom to" can always be reduced to or translated into cases of "freedom from." (E.g., if I am free to do my homework, I am free from any kinds of constraints which might have prevented me from doing it.)

It may be unfortunate that there is no necessary connection between "freedom" and engaging in valuable activities, but it seems to be preferable to recognize this than to suggest that the concept implies things which it does not imply. We do need to justify imposing constraints on children in schools, but an analysis of the concept of "freedom" does not lead us towards the required justifications. It is only by twisting the meaning of freedom that we can refer to constraining children as "freeing" them. In the previous section we argued that it may often be necessary to constrain children in schools and we defended this position by referring to the intrinsic value of the

[10] Cranston, *Freedom: A New Analysis*, p. 4.

development of rationality and understanding and the need which may arise to exert authority and impose constraints in order to lead children to what is worthwhile.

It has recently been argued by M. J. Charlesworth that the state's right to ensure that children receive education (though not its right to *provide* education) is to be justified on the basis that education is the *sine qua non* for the full exercise of liberty. In Charlesworth's view

> . . . education is necessary if people are to be capable of making their own decisions on personal values, and thus to become independent of the paternalistic guidance of the state . . . There is, then, nothing paradoxical in the state interfering with the liberty of parents and children (by insisting that children be educated) in order to more fully promote their liberty from state interference.[11]

Certainly there is nothing paradoxical in this, since it is not being implied that the interference *means* promotion of liberty. However Charlesworth's argument reintroduces a "means-end" model of education. Education is seen as instrumental to the promotion of liberty. We argued earlier that education necessarily increases people's capacity to make judgments over a wide variety of fields, including personal values. This growth of understanding is not something extrinsic to engaging in such activities as science and history; it is part of what is meant by engaging in them. We obviously ought to be pleased if an end result of such activities is that people's liberty from state interference is increased and this would in turn operate as a powerful motive for promoting education. But to see such results of education as aims of education perpetuates an instrumental view of education.

In Charlesworth s view education is not intrinsically valuable. On the contrary, he sees education as inevitably concerned with the transmission of value-judgments derived from personal "world views." Children have to be committed to

11 Charlesworth, M. J., "The Liberal State and the Control of Education," in Selleck, R. J. W., *Melbourne Studies in Education, 1967* (Melbourne: Melbourne University Press; London and New York: Cambridge University Press, 1968) p. 24.

some set of values by someone acting on their behalf. According to Charlesworth, only parents have the right to make such value decisions for the child and to educate them on the basis of these decisions

> . . . the parents must so educate the child that he is eventually in a position to make his own free personal commitment for or against the "world-view" in which he has been brought up. This is, after all, the difference between education in the true sense and indoctrination or "brain-washing."[12]

For Charlesworth, then, education is inevitably biased. All we can hope for, as we pass on our personal "world views" to our children is that they remain capable of choosing an alternative set of values to the ones we have transmitted. It is this liberty to decide and choose for oneself which is the overriding value, an intrinsic good, and education is instrumental to its achievement.

We must combat Charlesworth's view that our account of education as the development of understanding through the various forms of knowledge necessarily involves a more or less arbitrary commitment to values which might legitimately be rejected by those we educate. Charlesworth argues this as follows:

> It is no doubt true that education is concerned with training in basic intellectual skills and that in this it is governed by standards of intellectual objectivity which everyone must accept, irrespective of his personal values or "world-view." There is not a Catholic or Protestant or Humanist or Communist "line" in science or mathematics or even in history and literature. In the same way there is not a Catholic or Protestant or Humanist or Communist education; there is simply education. However, value judgements do not enter into education merely through the explicit teaching of religion and morals; they are also implied by the manner in which an education system is framed. If individual disciplines are considered separately, then the "neutralist"

12 Ibid., p. 25.

position just described can appear plausible. That two plus two equals four or that William the Conqueror landed in England in 1066 are truths that can be taught and appreciated independently of any assumptions. But an educational system is precisely a *system,* a corpus of disciplines with a rationale behind it. Certain subjects within the system are estimated to be more important than others and, in establishing this order of priorities, values are inevitably assumed. The topics selected for study in any subject (for instance, the choice of a particular period of history or of an author as being more relevant or important than another); the subjects held up as paradigms of knowledge; the intellectual, moral, social and aesthetic attitudes proposed, either deliberately or tacitly, to the pupils for emulation; the order of educational priorities established (whether, for instance, utilitarian subjects are given preference over the non-utilitarian); the way in which religion is seen as bearing upon other subjects (whether, for example, it is seen as a relevant part of the syllabus, or as a dispensable "extra-curricular" subject)—all these judgements will inevitably be influenced by the particular set of values that one espouses. Thus any educational system inevitably involves value assumptions which are in turn derived from a general "world-view."[13]

Let us consider these arguments separately:

(1) Why need certain disciplines be assumed to be more important than others? We have argued that with respect to their intrinsic value in the development of understanding, the various forms of knowledge cannot be compared since the only criteria we have for making judgments are contained within the various forms of knowledge themselves. If we hold up any discipline as a "paradigm of knowledge" we cannot imply that it is more valuable than another. There need be no value judgment involved in pointing out that judgments made by scientists usually relate to publicly accepted criteria in this domain in a way that is rarely so in literary criticism. When we suggested (in Chapter 3) that literary criticism might more appropriately be called a "form of discourse" rather than a

13 Ibid., pp. 18–19.

"form of knowledge" we did not imply that this necessarily meant that literary criticism is less valuable than science.

(2) While it is true that the topics selected for study within a discipline *may* reflect value judgments deriving from general "world views," this need not be so. Topics may surely be selected on educational grounds, e.g., "This period of history relates more closely to the experience or interests of the children," or "This poem introduces the children to a particular literary critical concept more effectively than that one."

(3) What are the "intellectual, moral, social and aesthetic attitudes" which are proposed, either deliberately or tacitly, to the pupils? How do these relate to "the manner in which an education system is framed?" Certainly if the framing of a system over-emphasizes one form of knowledge at the expense of another or stresses selected topics on noneducational grounds then attitudes may be formed which have their basis in a particular "world view." But we have just argued that these particular forms of bias are not inevitable in the framing of an education system.

(4) Education systems do differ with respect to the emphasis that is placed upon "utilitarian" subjects rather than "nonutilitarian" subjects. It does not follow, however, that such emphasis relates to a general "world view." In a country where there is a serious shortage of trained scientists we would expect the education system to concentrate upon the education of scientists, without assuming that the framers of the system thought science to be more important than other fields. Only if this emphasis continued when the deficiency had been made up would we have reason to suspect the system of pushing a particular "world view."

(5) The problems which arise with the teaching of religion are related to those which come up with the teaching of literary criticism. If there is religious knowledge then it must take its place in an education system alongside the other forms of knowledge. But as with literary criticism, many of the criteria for making judgments in this field are not publicly accepted, and many of the experiences (e.g., of God) which

are structured and organized in religious discourse seem not to be shared by everyone. To cope with these difficulties there should presumably be considerable diversity of provision in any education system, but it ought not to be assumed that any judgment that the framers of an education system make about the place of religious teaching in schools must derive from their particular "world views." It would be hoped that the diversity of educational provisions here would reflect the legitimate claims of each of the conflicting "world views" which enter into the debate about religious teaching.

Our conclusion is that Charlesworth has failed to characterize the introduction of children to the various forms of knowledge as being necessarily derived from certain "world views." If such bias were inevitable, then all education would be indoctrination in the sense we specified in Chapter 2. Bringing up children to accept our particular "world views" without regard for the truth of these views, is indoctrination—whatever hopes we may have that they will be free to "commit" themselves to alternative "world views" later on. We argued in Chapter 2 that it is often very difficult to decide on the truth of the beliefs and procedures which we teach but we concluded that this is a criterion which we must try to operate when we distinguish education from indoctrination.

Our conception of the content of education has been explicitly related to the criteria for truth in the various forms of knowledge. In education, only that which can be shown to be true according to these criteria may be passed on to children as true. So that when the state interferes with the freedom of parents and children in order to ensure that children are educated, it must also ensure that education does not become indoctrination. The state must ensure that what takes place in its schools does not involve the passing on of personal "world views." If this is ensured, we might more readily agree with J. S. Mill and M. J. Charlesworth that the state has the right to decide, both for children and parents, that education is such a great human good that no one shall choose not to be educated.[14]

[14] Ibid., pp. 22–23.

(C) EQUALITY AND EDUCATION

The main point which R. S. Peters wants to establish in his analysis of the concept of "equality" is that it indicates a certain kind of presumption in our treatment of people. As he says:

> No one should be presumed in advance of particular cases being considered to have a claim to better treatment than another.[15]

The onus is always on those who want to treat one person differently from another to justify the differences of treatment. What else can you do, rationally speaking, asks Peters, but treat people equally before you have reasons for differentiation of treatment?

Peter's argument stems from two main sources—Kant's moral views and K. R. Popper's argument in *The Open Society and Its Enemies*.[16] The ultimate justification for this view of equality is grounded in Kant's principles of impartiality and respect for persons.

Popper's main concern is to dispose of the view that equality is "natural." This is the sort of argument which lies behind those declarations of human rights which assert that all men are born free and equal. W. K. Richards' version in a book called *Education in the U.S.A.* takes the position to absurd lengths.

> We hold these truths as self-evident, that all men are created equal, that they are endowed by their Creator with certain inalienable rights, that among these are life, liberty, the pursuit of happiness and a high school diploma.

Popper rejects arguments based on biological naturalism on two grounds:

(a) First, he uses the Humean argument that evaluations cannot be derived from statements of fact. Even if it were true that men were born equal in some respect (e.g., their hu-

---

[15] R. S. Peters, *Ethics and Education*, p. 121. See also S. I. Benn and R. S. Peters, *Social Principles and the Democratic State*, Chapter 5.

[16] See particularly Chapter 5.

manity, their capacity to feel pain, etc.), it could not constitute a reason for treating them in one way or another, for this is a matter for a moral decision. As Popper points out, the decision to oppose slavery does not depend on the fact (if it is a fact) that all men are born free and equal. We could still try to put some in chains.

(b) Popper's main reason for opposing naturalist arguments for equality is his objection to Plato's use of naturalist arguments for inequality. Popper's book is largely an attack on Plato, and Popper is aware that to argue a case for equality on naturalist grounds is to play into the hands of Plato and anyone else who wants an elitist society. Plato made the standard objection to the naturalist arguments for egalitarianism—he pointed out that people are manifestly *not* equal and cannot be made so. According to Plato, men are born unequal both biologically and morally and the opposition between Greeks and barbarians corresponded to a *natural* division between masters and slaves. The natural inequality of men is one of their reasons for living together, says Plato, because their natural gifts are complementary. Against this theory of natural privilege *and* the theories of natural equality, Popper argues that both rest on the mistaken assumption that values are to be found in nature at all.

Popper's eagerness to expose Plato, however, leads him into certain important misinterpretations of the views of Plato and Aristotle. Plato and Aristotle's anti-egalitarianism is expressed most succinctly in the principle "It is unjust to treat unequals equally." Popper argues that it must be the principle of all morality that no man should consider himself more valuable than another person before any relevant reasons are produced. We have observed that this point is also made by Peters; but Popper's use of it here overlooks an important aspect of Aristotle and Plato's dictum. Popper assumes that what is meant is "It is unjust to treat inferiors equally." But "unequals" need not be inferiors—they may be superiors. We may regard someone as superior to ourselves in relevant respects and therefore qualified to lead us. Plato and Aristotle's dictum is not an elitist manifesto. It is the fundamental principle of justice. As such, it is open to many interpretations. Peters has pointed out that the original formulation ("It is un-just to treat unequals equally") might be taken as expressive of an emphasis on differentiation between people, as in the English educational system. Whereas the operative principle behind American education might be rather "It is just to treat equals equally," for American notions of justice and equality are much closer to the notion of treating people the same.

In fact, the current debate in American educational circles is on just this point. To what extent does the notion of equality imply that people be treated the same? Or should the principle of equality of treatment be interpreted as the principle of just or fair treatment? If the latter view is accepted, then cases where people are being treated differently may nevertheless be cases where they are being treated equally, on the grounds that they are being treated justly or fairly.

The fundamental objection to the view that treating people equally means treating them the same is that it may be unjust to treat people the same. If Johnny gets the same punishment as Billy when he breaks a school rule, although Johnny is a first offender and Billy has broken the rule several times before, the treatment is unjust and also, in an important sense, *unequal*. If 3A is taught in the same way as 3D, although 3A is composed of bright children and 3D of dull children, they have been treated the same, but one group has been treated unjustly. The point is an obvious one, of course. Treat-ing people equally may often imply treating them with equal regard to the differences between them and may thus imply treating them differently.

To what extent, then, are we to allow different treatment of people to be called equal treatment? This is the question which the American educational philosophers have been con-centrating upon.[17] They take the case of the two boys who receive different punishments for the same offense and point

---

[17] See, for example, B. Paul Komisar and Jerrold R. Coombs, "The Con-cept of Equality in Education" in *Studies in Philosophy and Education,* Vol. III, No. 3, Fall 1964, pp. 223–244. Also C. J. B. MacMillan, "Equality and Sameness," ibid., Vol. III, No. 4, pp. 320–26.

out that despite the difference in the treatment meted out, the boys are being treated the same in the sense that they both receive a penalty. It might be argued then, that unless the treatment under debate can be shown to be in some sense the same treatment, then it is inappropriate to speak of equal treatment. Thus, for example, if one of the boys broke the rule but was not penalized at all (because, for example, breaking the rule was necessary in order to save a teacher's life) we might say that he was treated justly, but we could not say that he was treated equally in relation to the boy who was penalized because there is no sense in which the treatment could be said to be the same in both cases.

At this point the notion of justice or fairness becomes separated from the notion of equality, with which it is customarily associated. The conclusion is that it is mistaken to refer to equality of treatment unless it is possible to describe the treatment as being the same in some relevant sense, i.e., a necessary element in the notion of equality is some relevant respect in which the treatment may be said to be the same. The catch, of course, comes with the idea of relevant sameness. If the teacher shouts angrily at one offender and speaks gently and encouragingly to another offender, it is possible to describe the treatment in each case as being the same in the respect that the teacher *spoke* to both offenders. But this is not a very relevant respect in this case. On the other hand the treatment of each offender may have been just or fair—the teacher may have behaved impartially towards each, for there may have been relevant differences between the two cases which justified the differences in the treatment. The shouting may have been justifiably provoked by a notorious nuisance and the gentle words may have been directed at someone who could not have been expected to know that he was committing an offense.

Both Peters' and Popper's accounts of equality are open to the objection that they are not really talking about equality but about justice or fairness. It need not be sufficient that one treat people fairly or justly or with impartiality if one is to treat them equally (although it is usually sufficient). It is necessary that one treat people impartially or fairly if he is to treat them equally. But it is also necessary that the treatment can be described as being in some sense the same treatment if it is to be a genuine case of equal treatment.

Bernard Williams[18] describes Peters' and Popper's sense of "equality" as the "weak sense." This weak sense is probably more appropriately called the principle of justice rather than of equality. In its weakest form it simply says that "reasons must be produced for treating people differently." But in this form it remains possible to say that the treatment which the slave traders meted out to Negroes was "just" because they produced reasons for it. So Williams suggests two additions to the weak form of the principle:

1. The reasons must be relevant ones.
2. The reasons must be socially operative.

The criterion of relevance is most difficult to assess as it requires moral argument. Slave traders may have claimed that certain alleged characteristics of Negro people were relevant grounds for treating them unequally. So we are pushed back to the foundations of ethics to combat their view. Only the merest reference to the relevant arguments can be made here. How, for example, would a slave trader meet the objection that he was treating Negroes as "means," not as "ends," in Kant's words? What "characteristics" of Negroes could be adduced which would be sufficient to lead us to treat them as less than "persons?" (For a penetrating analysis of the concept of a "person," see R. S. Peters' *Ethics and Education,* pp. 208–215). If the slave trader were to hold as a basic principle that Negroes are not persons and were just to leave it at that, then there would be little that we could say to him. But as in the case of Hitler and the Jews, such discrimination is usually argued by the discriminator. And, as Benn and Peters point out, this is to extend the principle of equal consideration to Jews and non-Jews, slaves and non-slaves alike. Benn and Peters continue by suggesting that the discriminator's argument is now vulnerable on several possible grounds:

[18] "The Idea of Equality" in *Philosophy, Politics and Society,* ed. P. Laslett and W. G. Runciman (Oxford: Basil Blackwell, 1964) p. 111.

(a) that the evidence will not support the claim that all Jews (Negroes, or women) are in the given respects inferior to non-Jews (white men, men);

(b) that the respects in which they do differ are irrelevant to some, if not all, of the forms of discrimination made to rest on them;

(c) where differences are relevant, the degrees of discrimination are out of all proportion to the degrees of difference.[19]

Williams' second addition to the weak form of the principle of justice was that the reasons for treating people differently must be socially operative. Without this addition equality may be merely "formal" and not "operative." For example, everyone is formally equal before the law. But there is frequently not operative equality, for if I have a lot of money, I can employ a better lawyer than a poor man. This distinction between formal and operative equality will be developed further in the next section with regard to equality of opportunity.

The following main points have been argued:

1. Men are not naturally either equal or unequal. Even if there were respects in which they were equal, it would require a further step to argue that they ought to be treated in any particular way.

2. It may be necessary to dissociate the principle of equality from the principle of justice. For in treating people fairly or justly, we may treat them so differently that there may be no respect in which the treatment may be said to be the same or even, similar. In such cases it would be inappropriate to speak of equal treatment.

3. When people have demanded equality they have usually been demanding justice. The principle of justice is, however, weak because it is a very general principle and it may be necessary to prop up the principle that "reasons be produced for treating people differently," by additional safeguards—that the reasons be relevant and socially operative.

[19] Benn and Peters, *Social Principles and the Democratic State,* p. 117.

(D) EQUALITY OF OPPORTUNITY
IN EDUCATION

Equality of opportunity is a principle which is invoked when access to goods or advantages which are in some way in limited supply is under consideration. Higher education, for example, is limited to people of certain ability, and since not everyone is able to partake of it, the notion of equal opportunity to do so is invoked. The principle has very wide currency in discussion of education today, and it is extremely rare to find anyone who is aware of the difficulties which are concealed by the principle. Its effectiveness as a slogan is indisputable. But as with slogans in general, the effectiveness is largely dependent on the illusion of false simplicity which it generates about matters which are extremely complex.

(a) Bernard Williams[20] points out that a thorough-going attempt to provide equality of opportunity involves a great deal of stress on the respects in which people are unequal; thus, for example, it stresses the differences in ability between people and it overstresses the value or worthwhileness of those jobs to which higher education provides access. If we have to go to great lengths to make sure that everyone has genuine equality of opportunity for higher education then we run the risk of devaluing those occupations which do not require higher education. And given that the former jobs are necessarily limited, the risks of spreading a sense of failure and inferiority among those who have not had higher education, and an elitism among those who have, must be balanced against the advantages of being meticulously fair in providing equality of educational opportunity.

(b) It may be necessary to treat people unequally in order to provide equality of opportunity. By this it is not meant merely that it may be necessary to treat people differently for as was argued in the previous section, treating people equally usually implies treating them differently (cf., Aristotle's point that it is unjust to treat unequals equally). Some advocates of equality of opportunity in education adopt the view that it may be necessary to take steps towards making children more

[20] "The Idea of Equality," *Philosophy, Politics and Society*, p. 124 et seq.

equal as a means of increasing their equality of opportunity, and this may involve not merely differentiation of treatment but unjust differentiation. We have already referred to sociological researches which suggest that "ability," as measured by intelligence tests, is to some extent a product of environmental factors, and may vary significantly in relation to social class. There can be little doubt that lower class children have less chance of succeeding in the tests taken by English children at eleven years of age[21] than do middle class children and this seems partly due to the relative cultural and linguistic impoverishment of lower class homes. The conclusion from this evidence is that there is not equality of opportunity *for* education or *in* education.

One solution to this problem is to provide "equality of opportunity" in the "strong" sense, i.e., to devote more resources to the education of lower-class children than to the education of middle-class children in an attempt to iron out the environmental advantages. This plan seems to be open to two objections. First it seems to be unjust to penalize the middleclass child for his advantages—it seems to make education into a "weight-for-ability" race—except that the penalty only comes if high abiltiy is associated with being middle class. (While there are good grounds for devoting a larger proportion of a nation's resources to the rehabilitation of a mentally or physically handicapped child, this is not, properly speaking, "education.") Second, social engineering is inappropriate *in* education. While education is, of course, a socializing force, it is a particular kind of socializing force. If education's distinctive concern with what is worthwhile and true is to be maintained, it must be denied that it can be used as a means of manipulating people toward any socially desirable end.

Nevertheless there is behind this advocation of a "strong" form of providing equality of opportunity an important point which ought not to be lost sight of. This is the recognition that an examination such as that taken by English children at eleven provides what might be called "formal" equality of

[21] The 11+ examination, for which a large proportion of English children sit, is partly an I.Q. test. Performance in this examination generally decides whether a child will enter a Grammar school or a Secondary Modern school. Few children from Secondary Modern schools enter universities.

opportunity for gaining a grammar school education; but this is not operative or actual equality of opportunity. It is equal opportunity in the sense that everyone takes the same test. But not everyone has had the same chances to gain the "ability" which the examination tests, and the lower-class child in particular is at a disadvantage in this regard. Similarly, if equality before the law is to obtain, then it is essential that everyone should have equal opportunity to acquire a good lawyer. If only wealthy people have the opportunity, then equality before the law is formal, not actual.

This distinction between "formal" and "actual" equality of opportunity is important, then, for it may direct attention to injustices which might otherwise go unrecognized. However in considering what ought to be done about making a formal provision actual, it becomes essential to consider the principle of equality in relation to other principles. It has been argued that an attempt to equalize children in education may be unjust and destructive of an adequate understanding of what "education" means. A single-minded concern with equality may also lead to the infringement of people's freedom. Sending slum children to boarding schools and raising the school leaving age are measures which may help to eliminate lower-class disadvantages. But at what point do these measures violate the freedom of parents to decide what is best for their children?

It would probably be better to defer selection in education until about 17 years of age, when much of the environmental disadvantages of lower-class children will have been overcome. In saying this, however, one is aware that the criteria for what is to constitute actual equality of opportunity in education are very slippery. In America, it is accepted in a number of quarters that everyone should have equal opportunity for a college education. And there is no doubt that what is meant is operative or actual equality of opportunity. Lieberman reports that in some colleges there is a system which allots marks in relation to ability. So that if a dull child is to get A, he need only score say 50% whereas a bright child may need to score 90% to get A. In advocating the replacement of formal equality of opportunity with operative equality of opportunity, it is essential that we steer well clear of trying to make people equal and of conjuring to equalize achievements.

The following difficulties with the concept of "equality of opportunity" have been identified:

1. By stressing the respects in which people are unequal and by stressing the desirability of certain occupations at the expense of other occupations, it seems likely that the advocation of equality of opportunity would lead many to feel that they had failed or were inferior. Equality of opportunity implies a highly competitive social and educational system, and competition has many disadvantages as well as advantages.

2. Equality of opportunity may be unobtainable unless the attempt is made to make people equal. This may involve injustice towards those who enjoy certain kinds of advantages, for example, those that stem from an advantageous upbringing. If the equalizing is to take place *in* education, an instrumental view of educational activities is unavoidable.

3. Although there is much to be said for making merely "formal" equality of opportunity "actual," this may infringe upon other important values. The main challenge to the advocate of equality of opportunity is to ask him to establish what is an unfair advantage. If intelligence is referred to as an unfair advantage (because it is partially the product of unequal social conditions), we have good reasons for doubting whether this challenge has been met satisfactorily.

SECTION (A)

Basic References

BANTOCK, G. H., *Freedom and Authority in Education*. New York: Humanities Press, Inc., 1965.

PETERS, R. S., *Ethics and Education,* Chapter 9. London: Allen and Unwin, Ltd., 1966.

———, *Authority, Responsibility and Education,* Part I. London: Allen and Unwin, Ltd., 1959.

Further References

BARZUN, J., *The House of Intellect,* Chapters IV and V. London: Mercury Books, 1962.

* What are the connections between being "an authority" and being "in authority"? Of what significance are they for the authority of the teacher?

* . . . the freedom to perform various skills and to make sense of the world around us . . . springs from the acceptance of and submission to the authority inherent in the various branches of human learning. And it is a fact of human experience that the "subjects" within which, in the course of time, we learn to move with the greatest assurance and freedom are not necessarily those which we were at first most "interested" by or "enjoy". (G. H. Bantock, *Education and Values*, [London: Faber and Faber, 1965.] p. 100)

Discuss.

* Must authority reside in the teacher?

SECTION (B)

Basic References

BANTOCK, G. H., *Education and Values*, Chapter IV. London: Faber and Faber, 1965.

——, *Freedom and Authority in Education*, Chapter III.

CHARLESWORTH, M. J., "The Liberal State and the Control of Education," *Melbourne Studies in Education*, ed. R. J. W. Selleck, 1967.

CRANSTON, M., *Freedom: A New Analysis*, London: Longmans, 1967.

PETERS, R. S., *Ethics and Education*, Chapter VII.

Further References

MILL, J. S., *On Liberty*.

NEILL, A. S., *The Free Child*, London: Herbert Jenkins, 1953.

Essay/Discussion Topics

* Ought teachers be free to express their own opinions?

* Freedom is a peculiarly slippery concept . . . some breaches of freedom are necessary and desirable; but one need not confuse

the issue by saying that they are, in that case, not "really" breaches of freedom at all. It may be agreed, however, that my freedom is enlarged if the number of choices open to me is increased. It is in this sense that education may be said to increase freedom. If you make a child learn French verbs when he would rather be outside playing, you are certainly restricting his freedom (though quite justifiably) and it is nonsense to say that you are not. But you are also in a slightly different sense, enlarging his feedom, since your hope presumably is that at the end of the process, he will have French as well as English literature available to him, if he chooses to read it. The alternatives from which he may choose will then have been increased and to that extent, he will be more free than before. In what is perhaps the only defensible sense of Rousseau's phrase, he will have been forced to be free. (D. H. Munro, "Democracy and Education," *Studies in Democracy*, W. H. C. Eddy, et al. [Melbourne: F. W. Cheshire, 1966] p. 136)

Analyze this argument in detail. Is it valid?

SECTION (C)

Basic References

Peters, R. S., *Ethics and Education*, Chapter IV.

Popper, K. R., *The Open Society and Its Enemies*, Vol. I, particularly Chapter 5. Princeton: Princeton University Press, 1963.

Tawney, R. H., *Equality*, Chapter I. London: Allen and Unwin, 1952.

Williams, B., "The Idea of Equality," *Philosophy, Politics and Society*, ed. Laslett, P. and Runciman, W. G., 2nd series. Oxford: Basil Blackwell, 1964.

Further References

McCloskey, H. J., "Egalitarianism, Equality and Justice," *Australian Journal of Philosophy*, Vol. 44, No. 1, May, 1966.

Rawls, J., "Justice as Fairness," *Philosophy, Politics and Society*.

Essay/Discussion Topics

* Should all children be considered equal?

* What is the relation between justice and equality?

* If someone were to suggest that all children should have an equal education, what might he mean? In what ways could the various meanings conflict?

SECTION (D)

Basic References

CROSSLAND, C. A. R., "Some Thoughts on English Education," *Encounter*, July, 1961.

GRIBBLE, J. H., "Equality of Opportunity in Education," *Education for Teaching*, February, 1966.

WILLIAMS, B., "The Idea of Equality," *Philosophy, Politics and Society*.

Further References

LIEBERMAN, M., "Equality of Educational Opportunity," *Language and Concepts in Education*, ed. Smith, B. O. and Ennis, R. H.

YOUNG, M., *The Rise of the Meritocracy*, London: Thames and Hudson, 1958.

Essay/Discussion Topics

* Should all children be given equal opportunity for education?

* Of what significance in a social and educational context is the distinction between formal and operative equality of opportunity?

* "Every child should have the same opportunity for *acquiring* measured intelligence." (R. H. Crossman)

Discuss.

7

The
Nature
of
Educational
Theory

OUR CONTROLLING CONCERN IN THIS BOOK has been with the meaning of some key terms in educational debate and with the logic of the justifications offered for a variety of views and policies in education. It is a peculiarity of philosophical discourse that it analyzes arguments in other forms of knowledge. In this section we will be pointing out that it also makes contributions to knowledge of its own; there is, however, an important respect in which philosophy is parasitic on other disciplines. It is not inaccurate to refer to this aspect of educational debate as "talk about talk," for this is a way of describing its second order character. Since psychology is of key importance in educational debate, it is not surprising that much of the work to be undertaken by educational philosophers is parasitic on psychology of education. When we think of the mass of psychological literature on child development and the nature of learning and motivation, we realize that we have made only a few introductory forays into the field in this book.

Neverthless it seems fitting that we should conclude by extending the range of our second order concerns by standing off from the particularities of educational controversy in order to ask what are the distinctive logical characteristics of the controversy itself. Oakeshott's supposition that "the diverse idioms of utterance which make up human intercourse have some meeting place and compose a manifold of some sort"[1] led him to the image of a "conversation" between the various "voices" of mankind rather than an "inquiry" or an "argument." While this image may be appropriate for the total impression given by all the various language-games that man plays, it is plain that the particular meeting place of the several voices of psychology, history, philosophy and sociology which contribute to form the bulk of educational controversy is very much an "argument." But it is often a confused and confusing argument. Oakeshott tries to reduce the confusion in the general "conversation of mankind" by rapping the knuckles of those who speak out of turn or who dominate the conversation so that others cannot be heard. At a number of points in the preceding chapters we have taken educational scientists to task for such lapses—in particular when they take it upon themselves to tacitly or explicitly make undefended value judgments. We have denied that such judgments fall within the realm of sociological or psychological discourse and have shown that educational psychologists and sociologists take some careful watching if we are not to be inveigled into accepting a variety of recommendations about what is worthwhile or what ought to be done. We have insisted that the philosopher has a distinctive contribution to make to such discussions, though we want to avoid the suggestion that the philosopher of education is responsible for deciding what ought to be done. Rather, it is the administrator, the headmaster, and above all the teacher himself who makes the decisions about what ought to be done in education in the light of his knowledge of his own subject and his acquaintance with the variety of arguments and evidence offered by educa-

[1] Michael Oakeshott, "The Voice of Poetry in the Conversation of Mankind," in *Rationalism in Politics and Other Essays* (London: Methuen, 1962) pp. 197–98.

tional psychologists, philosophers, historians and sociologists.

There can be no doubt that the scientific voices have predominated and that these are the ones that ring in teacher's ears (if any do at all!). Oddly enough there are a number of educational philosophers who seem not merely to acquiesce in this but who actually seek to justify it. We will begin by describing this phenomenon and then try to point out the misconceptions which produced it.

Professor Passmore would have us reject the term "educational theory" and refer to the entire realm of educational debate as "educational science." He describes this in Kingsley Price's words as

> The academic discipline that endeavours to understand the process by which the non-physical possessions of a culture —its skills, its arts, its knowledge—are transmitted and fostered in the rearing of the young and the instruction of adults.[2]

Passmore goes from this to claiming that educational science is "one of the social sciences and like any other science it needs to be firmly based on information about what actually happens." Educational science draws upon psychology, sociology and biology and it "stands in relation to teaching as horticultural science stands to gardening; it asks what goes on in our schools as horticultural science asks what goes on in our gardens." The remainder of Passmore's article, and much of the article which is a sequel to it, is devoted to an examination of the relationship between educational science and philosophy of education. And although it is difficult to determine exactly what is Passmore's view, he seems to come to the conclusion that philosophy of education is part of educational science. Thus, for example, he praises C. D. Hardie's *Truth and Fallacy in Educational Theory* because it has its eye on the need for establishing an educational science and "employs philosophy as an element, but only an element in that task."[3]

[2] J. A. Passmore, "Analytical Criticisms of Traditional Philosophies of Education," *Melbourne Studies in Education,* ed. E. L. French (Melbourne: Melbourne University Press, 1965) p. 56.

[3] Ibid., p. 64.

Although we would hold with Passmore and Hardie that it is important to "commingle" psychological and philosophical considerations in education, we think it is most misleading to view all theorizing and fact finding about education as educational science. One of Passmore's reasons for rejecting the inclusive term "educational theory" is that it is often used as a synonym for educational philosophy. Perhaps there is some risk of confusion here, but no one is likely to actually claim that educational philosophy is all there is to educational discussion, whereas some philosophers of education *do* hold the view that the *only* legitimate form of educational theory is scientific theory. Passmore is supporting this misconception. He seems to ally himself with the view of D. J. O'Connor, who maintains that

> . . . the word "theory" as it is used in educational contexts is generally a courtesy title. It is justified only when we are applying well established experimental findings in psychology or sociology to the practice of education. And even here we should be aware that the conceptual gap between our theories and the facts on which they rest is sufficiently wide to make our logical consciences uneasy. We can hope that the future development of the social sciences will narrow this gap and this hope gives an incentive to developing these sciences.[4]

Israel Scheffler also inclines towards viewing the theory of education as scientific theory. Admittedly the article in which this tendency is apparent is concerned not with the nature of educational theory but with the question which is its title, "Is Education a Discipline?" Having argued that there is no one discipline of education, Scheffler makes a number of leading remarks about the sort of studies which would be of use for the formulation of principles relevant to our work as educators.

> As educators, we will continue to ask all sorts of questions arising in the course of our work . . . we ought not to isolate ourselves from attempts to formulate principles

---

[4] D. J. O'Connor, *An Introduction to the Philosophy of Education* (London: Routledge and Kegan Paul, Ltd., 1966) p. 110.

relevant to our work, no matter what their disciplinary labels. . . . Rather, we should encourage relevant investigations by psychologists, anthropologists, sociologists, economists, educationists, and still others, and we should strive to link them with the concerns of schooling.[5]

Apart from the mysterious phrase "educationists and still others," the formulation of principles relevant to the educator's work seems to be viewed as the job of the social scientist. And this impression is reinforced by the whole emphasis of Scheffler's conclusion.

A crucial issue, it seems to me, is whether we can establish reliable principles to explain how and why children learn, schools develop, curricula change, ideals conflict, perceptions alter, societies differ, standards of taste and culture are formed. That *any* discipline is likely to be developed capable of answering these questions systematically and reliably is still a matter of some controversy. Ernest Nagel, a distinguished student of logical and methodological issues in the social sciences, has recently written that "In no area of social inquiry has a body of general laws been established comparable with outstanding theories in the natural sciences in scope of explanatory power or in capacity to yield precise and reliable predictions . . . many social scientists are of the opinion, moreover, that the time is not yet ripe even for theories designed to explain systematically only quite limited ranges of social phenomena. . . . To a considerable extent, the problems investigated in many current centres of empirical social research are admittedly problems of moderate and often unimpressive dimensions. . . . In short, the social sciences today possess no wide-ranging systems of explanation judged as adequate by a majority of professionally competent students, and they are characterized by serious disagreements of methodological as well as substantive questions.[6]

Scheffler remarks that the problem is thus to advance the state of social inquiry. What is astonishing about all this is the

[5] Israel Scheffler, "Is Education a Discipline?" in *Philosophy and Education*, ed. Israel Scheffler, Second Edition (Boston, Allyn and Bacon, Inc., 1966) p. 77.
[6] Ibid., p. 76.

extent to which the implicit assumptions coincide with those of O'Connor—that the formation of principles for educational practice is envisaged as the concern of scientists and scientific method. In Scheffler's case it seems even to have obscured his view of the sorts of "questions which arise in the course of the educator's work." The list of questions he offers is composed entirely of empirical questions about *how* or *why* children learn, schools develop and so on. O'Connor at least acknowledges that many different sorts of questions arise, to do with "aims" and what is worthwhile and a variety of questions about meaning. He simply limits the meaning of educational theory to include only those questions which are susceptible to scientific investigation. Scheffler does not even consider such questions as, "What ought children learn?" "How have schools developed in the past and how ought they develop in the future?" "In what direction have curricula changed and in what direction ought they to change?" "What standards of taste and culture do we want to pass on to children?" "What is meant by 'taste' and 'culture'?" "What do we mean by 'learning'?" and so on. Such philosophical and historical questions arise frequently in the course of an educator's work, and the attempt to answer them systematically in philosophy of education and history of education is surely a part of the theory of education. Similarly, these disciplines are often crucial components of the hybrid arguments which lead to the educational principles relevant to our work. Consider, for example, the way in which we balanced considerations from psychology, sociology and philosophy in our previous discussion of the use of intelligence tests in educational selection. Sociological evidence to the effect that middle-class children have an advantage over lower-class children in their performance on intelligence tests needs to be weighed against psychological evidence that intelligence tests are the best available discriminators of I.Q. at certain ages. And this in turn must be seen in relation to arguments of a philosophical and historical kind about the *desirability* of using such tests in educational selection.

In direct conflict with O'Connor and Scheffler is the view of P. H. Hirst, who holds that educational theory is characterized by its prescriptive function—educational theory is all the theory which is drawn upon in making recommendations for educational practice. Hirst distinguishes between what he calls "fields of knowledge" and "practical theories." He denies that educational theory is concerned "simply with collecting knowledge about practical affairs." In his view, "the whole point is the use of this knowledge to determine what should be done in educational practice."[7] He contrasts such a practical theory with a "field of knowledge," which is an "artificial unit" centering around some kind of object, phenomena, abstract entity or other interest, e.g., "the modern European mind," "the neighborhood," or "power." Such fields of knowledge might be developed for teaching purposes. And a subject like geography, centering on an interest in "man and his environment" is a "field" rather than a distinct "form of knowledge," lacking as it does distinctive concepts and distinctive criteria for making distinctive judgments. The geographer is "necessarily involved in employing the canons and methods of several different forms of knowledge, those, for example, of the historian, the economist, the physicist, etc."[8]

Educational theory is not a "field of knowledge," in Hirst's account, even though knowledge is collected from different forms of knowledge because of a particular interest. For, he says,

> the whole point is the use of this knowledge to determine what should be done in educational practice. . . . the whole raison d'être of a practical theory is its practical function.[9]

While Hirst's account is more satisfactory than the others we have examined, since it enables us to take into account the contribution of all the relevant disciplines which contribute to educational theory, it is far from clear that educational theory is bound to be relevant to the formulation of principles for

---

[7] P. H. Hirst, "Educational Theory," *The Study of Education,* ed. J. W. Tibble (London: Routledge and Kegan Paul, Ltd., 1966) p. 48

[8] Ibid., p. 47.

[9] Ibid., p. 48.

educational practice. Much of the theory is (quite legitimately) devoted to the development of understanding of educational matters for its own sake. The knowledge must, of course, have some bearing on educational matters—education is the "selected topic," just as "the modern European mind" may be the focus of another field of knowledge. In our view, much educational theory exhibits the characteristics of a field of knowledge, much of it is speculative rather than practical. Some of the knowledge gained will be used to provide the basis of justification for the formation of educational principles. But it is by no means the whole point of gaining knowledge about education that it be utilizable towards this end. It would certainly be logically neater if educational theory could be said to have the necessary logical characteristics of a practical theory as Hirst defines it. But it seems quite arbitrary to maintain that the logic of the whole activity is to be characterized by the logic of some of its parts.

Consider, for example, the instance which Hirst puts forward:

> The educationist is not simply interested in, for instance, the nature of historical explanation, the place in it of moral judgements, and the psychological aspects of acquiring historical concepts. He is concerned with using these kinds of knowledge to form rationally defensible principles about the place of history teaching in education, what history should be taught in schools and how it ought to be done.[10]

Hirst speaks here of what the "educationist" is interested in rather than of the educational *theorist's* interests. If the "educationist" is a practitioner, the practical implications of speculation on the nature of historical explanation will naturally be his primary interest. And of course it would be unlikely that such speculation would be without implications for educational practice. However, educational theorists frequently do not pursue their analyses into the formation of principles for educational practice and Hirst's reasons for thinking that they do so (or ought to do so) are obscure.

[10] Ibid., p. 48.

Would Hirst see his own article as being a contribution to educational theory? It seems to be ruled out by his own account of the nature of educational theory. He is not concerned with the formation of rationally defensible principles about what ought or ought not be done under the name of educational theory. His insistence throughout is on what the educational theorist *is* or *is not* interested in, not what he ought to be interested in. There might be a lot of practical value in arguing that educational theorists ought to be more concerned with educational practice, given the tendency of specialists in philosophy, psychology, sociology and history of education to cultivate their own little theoretical garden of understanding. One suspects that under the guise of analyzing the logical characteristics of educational theory, Hirst is in fact tacitly *recommending* a practical direction for the diverse forms of theorizing that go to make up educational theory, that he is tacitly making the moral judgments which he holds to be an essential part of educational theory. The paradox of his article is that he does not explicitly practice what he preaches. He passes up the opportunity to make strong practical recommendations and adopts instead the procedures of the analyst detached from the sound and fury of practical affairs. In this respect his article is a contribution to educational theory only if the theory is conceived of (at least partially) as a "field of knowledge." It appears to be concerned simply with increasing understanding of what educational theory *is*. The article falls short of educational theory in Hirst's own sense of it as a "practical theory" since it is not concerned with making practical judgments. Since there is a vast amount of theorizing which shows the ostensible concern of Hirst's article, i.e., simply to increase understanding of matters connected with education, it must surely be denied that Hirst offers an accurate description of the logical characteristics of educational theory.

Our contention that educational theory exhibits characteristics of a practical theory and of a field of knowledge does not necessarily have the consequence of conceiving the range of the theory to be more far-reaching. The limitations which would operate on the extent to which moral reasoning in education, for example, would be concerned with high-level statements about what is good or what ought to be done in general are limitations which would still be operative even if we conceive educational theory as partially a field of knowledge. If the interest in education as the focus of the "field" is to be retained, the moral philosopher in education will be limited mainly to specifically educational issues. It is not a contingent matter that the researches of educational psychologists, sociologists, etc., are concerned with educational matters—such a concern is necessary if the researches are to be in psychology of education or sociology of education. Whereas it seems to be a purely contingent matter whether or not these researches are in fact used to construct principles for educational practice. The possibility that the knowledge at which the educational theorist arrives after his labors in the lab or the armchair may be used to form practical principles by administrators or teachers need not control the direction of his labors.

We are far from disagreeing with Hirst's emphasis on the importance of the practical function of the theory. We have made every effort throughout this book to bring out the practical relevance of our theorizing. Hirst's concluding sentences are apposite in a situation where educationalist theorists are tending more and more to cultivate their theoretical interests in an insular fashion both in their research and their teaching.

> If we can begin to understand more accurately than in the past the way in which such fundamental disciplines as history, psychology, sociology and philosophy can in fact contribute to the rational determination of educational practice, then there is serious hope that the study of education by intending teachers will in future bear much greater practical fruit. That has been the aim behind this chapter . . .[11]

This has certainly been one of the aims behind this book, as well, though it has not controlled our discussions to the extent that we have ruthlessly eliminated reflections which seem to be important to our understanding of an educational issue rather than to our practice as teachers or administrators.

[11] Ibid., p. 57.

In this chapter we have argued that educational theory embraces more than scientific theory and includes various sorts of philosophical and historical investigation. Our rather banal suggestion was that educational theory is that theory which has educational matters as its subject matter, regardless of what the contributory discipline is. While much of the theorizing is concerned with the formation of practical principles, it is not exclusively prescriptive, for a legitimate concern of an educational theorist is with the development of understanding of some educational matter without necessarily any reference to the practice of education.

BASIC READING

HIRST, P. H., "Educational Theory," *The Study of Education*, ed. J. W. Tibble, London: Routledge and Kegan Paul, Ltd., 1966.

O'CONNOR, D. J., *An Introduction to the Philosophy of Education.* London: Routledge and Kegan Paul, Ltd., 1966.

PASSMORE, J. A., "Analytical Criticisms of Traditional Philosophies of Education" and "Towards an Analytic Philosophy of Education" in *Melbourne Studies in Education 1965*, ed. E. L. French, Melbourne: Melbourne University Press, 1965.

SCHEFFLER, I., "Is Education a Discipline?" *Philosophy and Education*, ed. I. Scheffler, Boston: Allyn and Bacon, Inc., 1966.

Walton, J. and Kuethe, J. L., *The Discipline of Education.* Madison, Wis.: Univ. of Wisconsin Press, 1963.

ESSAY/DISCUSSION TOPICS

* Is education a discipline?

* P. H. Nowell-Smith (*Ethics*, [Oxford: Blackwell, 1957] p. 11) distinguishes between theoretical and practical discourse by saying that the former "enables us to understand the nature of things, whether the things be stars, chemical substances, revolutions, or human behaviour." Whereas practical discourse "consists of answers to practical questions of which the most important is, 'What shall I do?' and 'What ought I to do?'" Examine any of the chapters in this book in order to elucidate the relationship which is implied between what is understood about human behavior and what ought to be done in education.

* How "practical" ought philosophy of education be? Has this book been too "practical" or not "practical" enough?

Appendix

FURTHER READING ON "SUBJECT PHILOSOPHY"

Philosophy of History

BURSTON, W. H. and THOMPSON, D., *Studies in the Nature and Teaching of History*, London: Routledge and Kegan Paul, Ltd., 1967.

DRAY, W., *Laws and Explanation in History*, London: Oxford University Press, 1960.

GALLIE, W. B., *Philosophy and the Historical Understanding*, New York: Schocken, 1964.

GARDNER, P., *The Nature of Historical Explanation*, Oxford: Oxford University Press, 1952.

MEYERHOFF, H. (ed.), *The Philosophy of History in Our Time*, Garden City, New York, Doubleday, 1959.

WALSH, W. H., *An Introduction to the Philosophy of History*, London: Hutchinson & Co. (Publishers) Ltd., 1951.

Philosophy of Literary Criticism

BUCKLEY, V., *Poetry and Morality*, London: Chatto, 1959.

CASEY, J., *The Language of Criticism*, London: Methuen, 1966.

Critical Moment, The, London: Forbes, 1964.

GARDNER, HELEN, *The Business of Criticism*, Oxford: Oxford University Press, 1963.

HARDING, D. W., *Experience into Words*, London: Chatto, 1963.

LANGER, SUSANNE, *Feeling and Form*, London: Routledge, 1959.

RIGHTER, W., *Logic and Criticism*, London: Routledge, 1963.

WIMSATT, W. K. and BEARDSLEY, M. C., *The Verbal Icon*, Lexington, Kentucky: University of Kentucky Press, 1954.

WITTGENSTEIN, L., *Lectures and Conversations on Aesthetics etc.*, Oxford: Blackwell, 1966.

Philosophy of Science

HARRE, R., *An Introduction to the Logic of the Sciences*, London: Macmillan, 1960.

HEMPEL, C. G., *Philosophy of Natural Science*, Englewood Cliffs, New Jersey: Prentice-Hall, 1966.

MADDEN, E. H., *The Structure of Scientific Thought*, Boston: Houghton-Mifflin, 1960.

POPPER, K. R., *The Logic of Scientific Discovery*, London: Hutchinson, 1959.

SMART, J. J. C., *Between Science and Philosophy*, New York: Random House Inc., 1968.

TOULMIN, S., *The Philosophy of Science*, London: Hutchinsons University Library, 1953.

Index

Ennis, R. H., 61
Ends (*see* Aims, educational)
Equality, educational (*see also* Opportunity, equality of)
  discrimination, 170-71
  formal equality, 171, 173-74
  impartiality principle, 166-71
  justice, 168-71
  Naturalism, 166-68
  operative equality, 170-71, 173-74
Ethics (*see* Moral judgments)
Experience, structuring of, 9-11, 48-49, 56, 77-78 (*see also* Knowledge, forms of)
Extrinsic value, 7-11, 43-49, 152, 161-65 (*see also* Aims, educational)

Facts, 25, 57, 59, 64-70
Fields of knowledge (Hirst), 185-88
Fisher, Mark, 93-94
Fleming, C. M., 81
Foot, Philippa, 123-29
Forms of knowledge (*see* Knowledge, forms of)
Freedom, educational:
  constraint, 157-70
  government responsibility, 161, 165
  liberty, 161-62
  limitations of, 157-61
  personal world view, 161-65
Freedom from; Freedom to (Cranston), 157-61
Freudian psychology, 38-39

Gardner, P., 51-52
Gasking, D. A. T., 12
Geach, Peter, 61-62
Generalization, 51-54
Getzels, J. W., 99-102
Giles, H. H., 81
Growth, personal, 76-80 (*see also* Self-realization)
Guilford, J. P., 97

Hadow Report of 1931, 25, 64
Hardie, C. D., 181
Hare, R. M., 36-37, 120, 123-25
Harding, D. W., 154
Hartman, G. W., 75, 105
Hirst, P. H., 47-49, 185-88

History, 42-44, 46, 51-56, 68-69 (*see also* Knowledge, forms of)
History, theories of:
  conceptual uniqueness, 51-56
  scientific history, 51-53
Horrocks, J. E., 80-81, 85
Hospers, John, 110-16, 119, 142-43
Hudson, Liam, 102, 108
Hull, Clark, 28
Hume, David, 121-23, 166-67

Imitation, 25
Impartiality, principle of, 125-29, 134-35, 166-71
Indoctrination, 16, 18-22, 29-40, 153, 162, 169
  alteration of beliefs, 29-30
  forms of knowledge, 33-34, 36-39
  independent judgment, 35
  isolated belief, 31-32
  non-doctrinal sense of, 30-40
  moral education, 123
  public verification of truth, 33-36, 39
  rational understanding, 18-20
  set of beliefs, 20, 29-34, 36, 38-40
Infinite regression, 45
Instruction:
  caring, 24
  moral education, 129, 131, 133, 136
  skill, 24-25
  teaching method, 18
Intelligence:
  behavior, 87
  imagination, 96-104
  intention, 89-90
  learning ability, 90-95
Intelligence Quotient Test (*see also* Creativity tests)
  convergent thinking, 102
  innate learning ability, 86, 90-93
  intellectual performance, 95-96
  low learning capacity, 93-95
  middle class, 92, 184
  opportunity and, 173
  remedial treatment, 93-95
Intrinsic value, as education criterion, 7-11, 17, 43-49, 103, 152, 160-63
Ipcress File, The, 29